Writing the Critical Essay

Racial Profiling

An OPPOSING VIEWPOINTS® Guide

Lauri S. Scherer, *Book Editor*

OPPOSING
VIEWPOINTS®
SERIES

GREENHAVEN PRESS
A part of Gale, Cengage Learning

GALE
CENGAGE Learning®

Detroit • New York • San Francisco • New Haven, Conn • Waterville, Maine • London

Elizabeth Des Chenes, *Director, Publishing Solutions*

© 2012 Greenhaven Press, a part of Gale, Cengage Learning

Gale and Greenhaven Press are registered trademarks used herein under license.

For more information, contact:
Greenhaven Press
27500 Drake Rd.
Farmington Hills, MI 48331-3535
Or you can visit our Internet site at gale.cengage.com

For product information and technology assistance, contact us at

Gale Customer Support, 1-800-877-4253
For permission to use material from this text or product, submit all requests online at www.cengage.com/permissions

Further permissions questions can be e-mailed to permissionrequest@cengage.com

Articles in Greenhaven Press anthologies are often edited for length to meet page requirements. In addition, original titles of these works are changed to clearly present the main thesis and to explicitly indicate the author's opinion. Every effort is made to ensure that Greenhaven Press accurately reflects the original intent of the authors. Every effort has been made to trace the owners of copyrighted material.

Cover image © Bruce Adams/Daily Mail/Rex/Alamy.

LIBRARY OF CONGRESS CATALOGING-IN-PUBLICATION DATA

Racial profiling / Lauri S. Scherer, book editor.
   p. cm. -- (Writing the critical essay: an opposing viewpoints guide)
Includes bibliographical references and index.
ISBN 978-0-7377-5913-6
1. Racial profiling in law enforcement. I. Scherer, Lauri S.
HV7936.R3R35 2012
363.2'3089--dc23

                                                              2011052233

Printed in the United States of America
1 2 3 4 5 6 7 16 15 14 13 12

CONTENTS

Examining the state of writing and how it is taught in the United States was the official purpose of the National Commission on Writing in America's Schools and Colleges. The commission, made up of teachers, school administrators, business leaders, and college and university presidents, released its first report in 2003. "Despite the best efforts of many educators," commissioners argued, "writing has not received the full attention it deserves." Among the findings of the commission was that most fourth-grade students spent less than three hours a week writing, that three-quarters of high school seniors never receive a writing assignment in their history or social studies classes, and that more than 50 percent of first-year students in college have problems writing error-free papers. The commission called for a "cultural sea change" that would increase the emphasis on writing for both elementary and secondary schools. These conclusions have made some educators realize that writing must be emphasized in the curriculum. As colleges are demanding an ever-higher level of writing proficiency from incoming students, schools must respond by making students more competent writers. In response to these concerns, the SAT, an influential standardized test used for college admissions, required an essay for the first time in 2005.

Books in the Writing the Critical Essay: An Opposing Viewpoints Guide series use the patented Opposing Viewpoints format to help students learn to organize ideas and arguments and to write essays using common critical writing techniques. Each book in the series focuses on a particular type of essay writing—including expository, persuasive, descriptive, and narrative—that students learn while being taught both the five-paragraph essay as well as longer pieces of writing that have an opinionated focus. These guides include everything necessary to help students research, outline, draft, edit, and ultimately write successful essays across the curriculum, including essays for the SAT.

Using Opposing Viewpoints

This series is inspired by and builds upon Greenhaven Press's acclaimed Opposing Viewpoints series. As in the parent series, each book in the Writing the Critical Essay series focuses on a timely and controversial social issue that provides lots of opportunities for creating thought-provoking essays. The first section of each volume begins with a brief introductory essay that provides context for the opposing viewpoints that follow. These articles are chosen for their accessibility and clearly stated views. The thesis of each article is made explicit in the article's title and is accentuated by its pairing with an opposing or alternative view. These essays are both models of persuasive writing techniques and valuable research material that students can mine to write their own informed essays. Guided reading and discussion questions help lead students to key ideas and writing techniques presented in the selections.

The second section of each book begins with a preface discussing the format of the essays and examining characteristics of the featured essay type. Model five-paragraph and longer essays then demonstrate that essay type. The essays are annotated so that key writing elements and techniques are pointed out to the student. Sequential, step-by-step exercises help students construct and refine thesis statements; organize material into outlines; analyze and try out writing techniques; write transitions, introductions, and conclusions; and incorporate quotations and other researched material. Ultimately, students construct their own compositions using the designated essay type.

The third section of each volume provides additional research material and writing prompts to help the student. Additional facts about the topic of the book serve as a convenient source of supporting material for essays. Other features help students go beyond the book for their research. Like other Greenhaven Press books, each book in the Writing the Critical Essay series includes bibliographic listings of relevant periodical articles, books, websites, and organizations to contact.

Writing the Critical Essay: An Opposing Viewpoints Guide will help students master essay techniques that can be used in any discipline.

Does Racial Profiling Help or Hinder Law Enforcement?

On July 22, 2011, a man named Anders Behring Breivik embarked on a carefully planned and chillingly executed terrorist attack in Norway. That afternoon, Breivik exploded a car bomb outside a government building in the capital city of Oslo, killing eight people. He then took a ferry to nearby Utoya Island, where he terrorized and killed dozens of young people who were at a politically oriented summer camp there. Breivik reportedly was dressed as a police officer and told the campers he had come to check on their security in the aftermath of the bombing in the capital. He gathered them together and for more than an hour, systematically shot them. Survivors reported that he delighted in hunting down those who tried to escape. He ultimately surrendered to police, but not until he had killed sixty-nine people, most of them teenagers.

Although the world was shocked by such a gruesome slaughter of young people, and by an act of graphic violence in an otherwise peaceful country, they were even more surprised when they learned what Breivik looked like. With blond hair, blue eyes, and skin so white it is nearly translucent, Breivik, who was born and raised in Norway, looked the very opposite of a "terrorist." As political analyst Yousef Munayyer puts it, "Breivik looks more like someone you might see hopping into a bobsled at the Winter Olympics, not the type you expect to see getting a thorough screening at the airport."[1]

That there is even such a notion of "what a terrorist looks like" is the exact idea underlying racial profiling, a controversial practice that seeks to identify law breakers—whether they be drug dealers, terrorists, or illegal immigrants—on the basis of whether they fit a profile of characteristics of people who tend to engage in a particular criminal activity. Profiling is based in part on stereotypes and in part on historical precedence, and although no study has ever proven its effectiveness, supporters find it hard to deny the seeming logic that if it is known that people from a specific group tend to commit a specific crime, it stands to reason that that group should be scrutinized more intensely than others. Opponents of racial profiling argue it is a discriminatory practice that presupposes innocent people of law breaking. They also say it is poor police work, claiming that if lawbreakers know police are mainly looking for one type of person, they will simply make themselves look different from the profile. In other words, focusing on a person who supposedly looks like a terrorist causes authorities to miss people who actually *are* terrorists.

That Anders Behring Breivik defied any profile appears to have helped him escape initial notice by Norwegian law enforcement. When the first reports came in of the bombing at the government office, officials may have rushed to conclusions about who the perpetrator was. Robert Parry is one columnist who pointed out that Breivik defied law enforcement's expectations of what a terrorist looks like so much that it may have even slowed down their search for him. "If the [known-to-be-conservative] Fox News promoters of racial profiling had been in charge of investigating last Friday's terror attack in Norway," said Parry, "they might well have encountered blond, blue-eyed Anders Behring Breivik and his two smoking-hot guns only long enough to ask if he'd seen any suspicious-looking Muslims around." People like Parry think it is wrong that conservative pundits and other supporters of racial profiling are so quick to believe that Muslims are the source of all terrorism, precisely because they will miss other people who pose a serious and deadly threat. "A clean-cut Nordic sort like Breivik," notes Parry, "is someone who would get a pass [if profiled]."[2]

That a white, blonde-haired, blue-eyed terrorist had perpetrated such a heinous crime profoundly struck the editors of the London newspaper the *Independent*, who wrote in the wake of the attacks, "Political violence is not the exclusive preserve of militant Islamists." It reminded them that overly focusing on some profiles "would represent a dangerous oversight."[3] Munayyer agreed and argued that Breivik single-handedly proved that racial profiling wastes money and resources and ultimately benefits no one's security. "There needs to be a serious rethinking about the Islamist boogeyman and a reevaluation of the share of security and intelligence resources dedicated exclusively to it," he wrote just days after the Norway attacks. "Breivik's ethnic background and the fact that he knew it would help him 'escape the scrutiny so often reserved for young men of Arab descent' should put to rest any discussion about racial profiling as an effective or efficient security measure, Munayyer concluded."[4]

But supporters of racial profiling claim there will always be a few exceptions to every rule, and they hold fast to the claim that, by and large, criminals—especially terrorists—tend to share a set of characteristics, national origins, and political and religious beliefs. To pretend otherwise is to deny reality, they say, at the expense of people's safety. "The current threat to passengers and airliners comes almost exclusively from one source, and we all know what it is," says conservative columnist Deroy Murdock, "young males between about 18 and 35 who practice a fundamentalist strain of the Islamic faith, and generally hail from the Middle East, as well as largely Muslim nations in Africa and South Asia."[5]

Murdock and others say that looking more closely at people who share such characteristics is sound police work and common sense. After all, Anders Behring Breivik and Timothy McVeigh (a white American who killed 168 people when he blew up the federal building in Oklahoma City in 1995) may defy the profile, but many other apprehended terrorists fit it perfectly. These would include Umar

Farouk Abdulmutallab, who in December 2009 tried to blow up a Detroit-bound plane with explosives hidden in his underwear; Najibullah Zazi, who sought to blow up the New York City subway in 2009; and Nidal Hasan, who killed twelve and wounded thirty-one in a November 2009 shooting spree at Fort Hood. "We are not arguing that the Transportation Security Administration should send anyone named Mohammed to be waterboarded [tortured] somewhere between the [airport's] first class lounge and the Pizza Hut," asserts Murdock. "However, if you are a male between about 18 and 35 and are traveling on a Middle Eastern passport or one from a predominantly Muslim country, it might be smart to ask you a few extra questions, carefully peruse your papers, and if things seem unusual we perhaps should take a closer look at your luggage."[6]

Whether racial profiling helps or hinders law enforcement remains a source of controversy and debate, even as the specifics of the debate shift from terrorism to illegal immigration and other illicit activity. These are among the many issues explored in the strongly argued viewpoints and model essays that compose *Writing the Critical Essay: Racial Profiling*. Readers will also consider arguments about whether racial profiling is unfair, violates rights, keeps people safe, or is a good use of limited resources. Thought-provoking writing exercises and step-by-step instructions help readers write their own five-paragraph expository essays on the topic.

Notes

1. Yousef Munayyer, "Lessons Drawn from the Blonde Bomber," Al Jazeera, July 26, 2011. http://english .aljazeera.net/indepth/opinion/2011/07/20117268 61255428.html.
2. Robert Parry, "Who Commits Terrorism?," OpEd News, July 27, 2011. www.opednews.com/articles/5/Who -Commits-Terrorism-by-Robert-Parry-110727-810 .html.

3. *Independent* (London), "A Massacre Born from a Poisonous Mindset," July 25, 2011.

4. Munayyer, "Lessons Drawn from the Blonde Bomber."

5. Deroy Murdock, "U.S. Airports Should Use Racial and Religious Profiling," Intelligence Squared U.S., Rosenkranz Foundation, November 22, 2010, p. 4. http://intelligencesquaredus.org/wp-content/uploads/airport-profiling-112210.pdf.

6. Murdock, "U.S. Airports Should use Racial and Religious Profiling," p. 4.

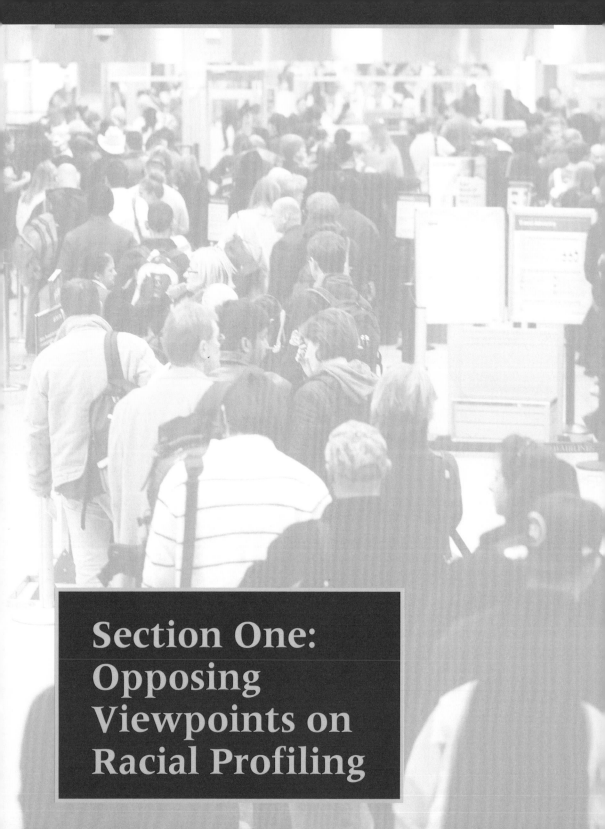

Section One:
Opposing
Viewpoints on
Racial Profiling

Racial Profiling Prevents Terrorism

C. Scott Litch

In the following essay, C. Scott Litch argues that the United States should use profiling to catch terrorists before they strike. He discusses the case of Israel, a frequent target of terror attacks. Israel uses profiling to catch people who seem likely to launch an attack; the United States, on the other hand, uses random screening procedures. In Litch's opinion, this makes no sense—the United States is a much larger country than Israel, and thus has millions more people to randomly sift through. This process wastes time and resources, in his opinion. Secondly, says Litch, America has been attacked predominantly by one type of person—Muslim men. Therefore, he says it is silly to waste time pretending that anyone might be a terrorist; since America knows it is typically attacked by Muslim men, it should focus its terror-screening resources on them. Litch concludes that racial profiling may not be politically correct, but it will save more lives and prevent more attacks than random screening procedures.

Litch, an attorney, is the author of *The Principled Conservative in the 21st Century*.

Consider the following questions:

1. How many people and international airports does the United States have compared with Israel, according to Litch?
2. What happened to the author's mother when she traveled to an assisted living facility?
3. What, according to Litch, would not "personally offend" him?

C. Scott Litch, "The Israelis Are Right: Profiling Makes Sense," *The Daily Caller*, January 13, 2011. http://dailycaller.com. http://www.facebook.com/profile.php?id =1492971497&ref = profile#!/pages/The-Principled-Conservative-in-21st-Century -America/154900131225397.

US Homeland Security Secretary Janet Napolitano visited Israel to study their airport security measures. She concluded that it would be impractical for the United States to adopt Israel's security system because the numbers of US airports and air travelers far exceeds those in Israel.

U.S. Homeland Security Secretary Janet Napolitano recently visited Israel to learn about Israel's airport security measures. She was quick to say, however, that Israel's security measures should not be adopted in America. Her reasoning? Israel has only 7.3 million people, while America has 310 million. Israel has only one major international airport and 11 million overall airline travelers each year, while America has 450 international airports and 70 times the number of airline passengers as Israel.

Random Screening Wastes Resources

Come again? Israel, with its much smaller numbers, relies heavily on behavioral profiling of travelers. America

Americans Support Racial Profiling

A 2010 *USA Today*/Gallup poll asked Americans whether airline passengers who fit a particular ethnic profile should be subjected to more intense security. The majority thought they should.

Question: "Some people have suggested that airline passengers who fit the profile of terrorists based on their age, ethnicity or gender should be subjected to special, more intensive security checks before boarding US flights. Do you favor or support this practice?"

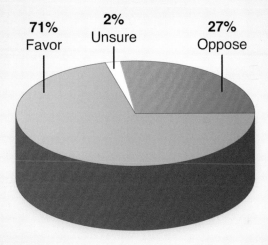

71%
Favor

2%
Unsure

27%
Oppose

Taken from: *USA Today*/Gallup poll, January 8–10, 2010.

rejects individual profiling and screens everyone? This seems wildly illogical. You would think that a country with a much smaller population might actually be able to screen EVERY passenger, whereas a country the size of America would use selective profiling so that its resources would not be stretched too thin. But it is just the opposite. America wastes tremendous time and resources on screening grandmothers. And yes, I take this personally, because it's hard for my family to forget the completely

Passengers stand in an airport security line in Tel Aviv, Israel. The Israeli security system has been frequently criticized for its use of individual profiling.

unnecessary extra screening applied to my 83-year-old mother (now deceased), who had Alzheimer's disease. She was subject to an extra search and questioning while en route to an assisted living facility. Will future generations praise us for authorizing such actions?

We Know Who to Focus On

Let's not beat around the bush here. The Israeli system is being rejected because it involves the politically incorrect tactic of individual profiling. So rather than risk offending a small number of Muslim men, we will operate in the dark even if it means more Americans will be killed by radical Islamic terrorists. Of course all Muslims are not potential terrorists. But to date 100% of such terrorists have been young Muslim men. Hence, they should logically be subject to greater scrutiny. I would say the same thing about profiling if there were a comparable terrorist movement organized by Jews, Christians, Hindus, or Buddhists. If thousands of bald Jewish men in their late 40s had formed a movement to destroy the useless airplane drink carts, I wouldn't be personally offended if I had to undergo a higher level of scrutiny when I passed through airport security checkpoints. The brief delays wouldn't be a huge inconvenience for me. Rather than be mad at the government, I would direct my anger towards the bald Jewish brigade.

> ## Focusing On the Most Suspicious People Is Effective and Efficient
>
> [The Israeli] system, the envy of many worldwide . . ., is often disparaged as "racial profiling," but it is what allows the great majority of passengers to be waved through after a quick conversation, and with considerably less inconvenience, humiliation and intrusion than frequently encountered in American airports. It also allows security personnel to focus on those who most arouse suspicion. Terror-prevention efforts are thereby rendered both more efficient and effective.
>
> *Jerusalem Post*, "Keep Our Airports Safe," March 9, 2011. www.jpost.com/Opinion/Editorials/Article .aspx?id = 211484.

Being Politically Correct

If America adopted logical security methods, we know the usual suspects would cry foul. They are more than welcome to issue press releases decrying the alleged human rights violations. We do have free speech in this country after all. However, until these same organizations write columns and issue press releases condemning terrorism and recognizing Israel's right to exist, we must also reserve the right to boldly ignore them.

Sadly, our current policy is a recipe for failure. I dread the day when a suspect who should set off all the bells and whistles breezes through a checkpoint while heterosexual male TSA [Transportation Security Administration] employees contemplate a full cavity search of [sexy pop star] Fergie.

Analyze the essay:

1. To make his argument in support of racial profiling, Litch says that, to date, 100 percent of terrorists that have attacked the United States have been young Muslim men, and thus the United States should focus on this group when looking for people who intend to harm Americans. How might other authors in this section—specifically Ahmed Rehab, Asra Q. Nomani, and Yousef Munayyer—respond to this claim and argument? Write one or two sentences for each author on whether terrorists who target America are solely young Muslim men. Then, state your opinion on the matter. Is it true that 100 percent of the people who have attacked the United States have been young Muslim men? Based on your answer, what approach do you think law enforcement should take when screening the public for terrorists?

2. Litch used facts, statistics, examples, and reasoning to make his argument that racial profiling can prevent terrorism. He does not, however, use any quotations to support his point. If you were to rewrite this article and insert quotations, what authorities might you quote from? Where would you place them, and why?

Racial Profiling Does Not Prevent Terrorism

Ahmed Rehab

In the following essay Ahmed Rehab argues that racial profiling does not prevent terrorism. He says terrorists are never caught by airport security officials who racially profile passengers. Rather, when terrorists are caught, it happens well before they get to the airport, through solid police work and intelligence. Therefore, security must be objective and steeped in science, intelligence, and technology, not something as subjective, emotional, and hasty as racial profiling. He also argues that racial profiling is too easy to beat—once terrorists know that officials are looking for one type of person, they will simply begin to change who they send. Racial profiling is a classic case of fighting the last battle, says Rehab. Law enforcement must not look for the type of person who committed the last terrorist attack but rather anticipate who will commit the next one. The best way to implement such a policy is to avoid racial profiling and rely on intelligence and technology.

Rehab is a columnist who writes about American Muslim affairs. He is the executive director of the Council on American-Islamic Relations–Chicago, a Muslim civil rights and advocacy organization.

Consider the following questions:

1. What clues should have tipped authorities off to the terrorist ambitions of Umar Farouk Abdulmutallab beyond his name and appearance, according to Rehab?
2. What two prominent individuals does the author say would likely be apprehended by security officials who rely on profiling?
3. What type of person blew up a Russian plane in 2004, according to the author?

Ahmed Rehab, "Why Racial Profiling Makes for Dumb Security," *Huffington Post*, January 7, 2010. http://www.huffingtonpost.com.

By now, I am sure most people are privy to the raging public debate on racial profiling, reignited courtesy of a young Nigerian Muslim male's attempt to detonate an incendiary device aboard a Detroit-bound Northwest flight last Christmas [2009].

After Umar Farouk Abdulmutallab slipped by airport security only to be stopped thanks to the vigilance of fellow passengers, a debate on the *effectiveness* of airport security and counter-terrorism intelligence is no doubt in order.

But trying to fix a problem without actually fixing the problem is misguided. Trying to fix it by introducing a new problem is dumb.

Legitimate Security Flags Were Missed

This guy seemed to have left every clue short of raising his hand and proclaiming, "Arrest me, I am a terrorist!"

Can someone explain to me how he managed to purchase a one way ticket, pay for it in cash, board the plane with no luggage, have his own father report him as a radicalized threat to a CIA base in Nigeria, be denied a visa to the UK where he previously lived and worked, and on top of that be on an active US terror watch list for two years, yet still not be flagged by the system as a security threat?

And can someone explain to me how after those six glaring red flags were missed—not to mention the explosive material in his underwear—the debate today is not about why and how they were missed, but about whether he could have been flagged for being of a certain skin color, hair texture, place of birth, faith, or namesake?

Racial Profiling Misses the Point

The racial profiling argument is lazy and unimaginative; most of all it is irresponsible because it evades the real problem staring us in the face: a fatal breakdown in communication between our intelligence units. Ironically, this

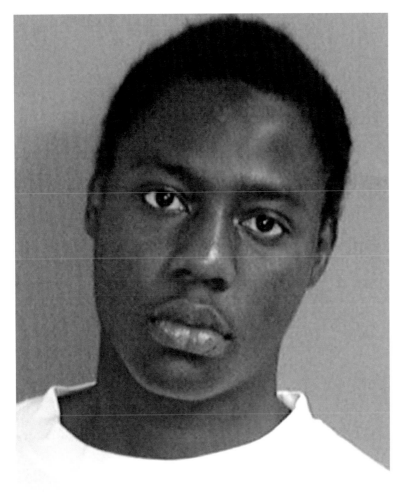

When would-be terrorist bomber Umar Farouk Abdulmutallab slipped through airport security, the vigilance of fellow travelers averted Abdulmutallab's terrorist act.

is a problem so troubling that an entire new department, the National Homeland Security Department, was created with the sole mission to address it.

Make no mistake about it; it is hardly ever a case of not having the necessary intelligence. Even in the case of the 9/11 hijackers, we had security files on each of the 19 hijackers. The problem is in our repeated failure to act upon intelligence between our fingertips in a timely manner. Introducing new and untested wild card measures will not correct what's failing, though the debate makes for a convenient distraction from bearing responsibility.

The idea that there are some racial profiles we need to check out thoroughly in order to conclusively determine that they do not have bombs on them is not what troubles me most. What truly troubles me is the corollary of that idea: that we know of a way to conclusively determine whether someone has a bomb on them or not but we are going to exempt most people from it because we do not deem them suspicious enough, or we do not have the resources for it. How is that supposed to make us feel safer?

Security Must Be Objective and Scientific

There is nothing comforting about a de facto admission by security officials that our primary airport security lines are a prop up [meant to give a false sense of safety] and that secondary ones are where it's really at. So, what's the point of primary security? Placebo? Clearly, what will make us safer is beefing up our primary security measures so that they actually do what they are supposed to do for the entire population (conclusively determine that no bombs or explosive material makes it through). It certainly isn't adding a secondary layer that, by design, most passengers will end up skipping. As good as that layer may be it won't be good enough, given that it is only partially applied to the passenger population.

Any security analyst will tell you that if we have a national security defense system that waits until an airport security gate to identify terrorists, then it's only a matter of time before it's good night and good luck. But even at security gates, our last-guard measures need to be scientific and objective, like improving bomb detecting machines; you know, the ones that

> ## Terrorists Will Simply Send People Who Differ from the Profile
>
> The [Transportation Security Administration] can't tell its employees never to give a pat-down to a 95-year-old woman, or a 6-year-old boy, or an adult who doesn't want anyone to touch his "junk"—to quote a couple of other embarrassing moments for airport screeners. Why? Because as soon as certain classes of people are identified as non-threatening, then terrorists are likely to recruit people who fit that exact profile.
>
> *Baltimore Sun*, "TSA: Treatment of Elderly Cancer Patient Raises Questions About Airport Screening," June 27, 2011. http://articles.baltimoresun.com /2011-06-27/news/bs-ed-pat-down-20110627 _1_pat-down-tsa-cancer-patient.

Profile Behavior Above Race

A 2010 *USA Today*/Gallup poll asked Americans what characteristics should be included in a security profile. The vast majority thought it was more important to profile behavior and travel history than race or religion, though slim majorities said nationality and personal appearance should be considered.

Question: "If profiling is done, for each item I name please tell me if you think it should or should not be included in a passenger's security profile. How about a passenger's:"

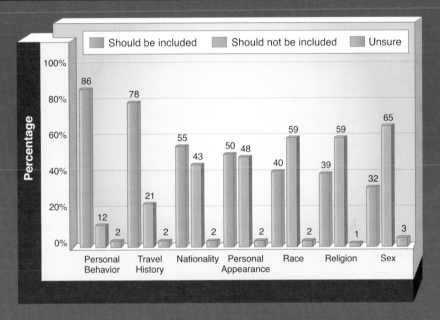

Taken from: ABC News/*Washington Post* poll, November 21, 2010.

didn't beep when dynamite underpants stepped through. Objective and scientific measures, however, do not include part-timers eyeballing passengers for people who look like characters out of Disney's *Aladdin* or whatever image their mind conjures of what a terror suspect looks like that day of the week.

According to many security analysts, a national security defense system that relies on identifying terrorists at airport security gates is an ineffective approach to safeguarding the country.

Targeting Both Jesus and Obama

So what *do* they look like? Presumably we are talking about Muslim men, but short of Muslims wearing green arm bands, what does that really mean?

Any Middle-Eastern looking person with an exotic sounding name?

Fine, this may work, provided we can count on Middle-Eastern terrorists with exotic sounding names being unaware of our little precautionary measure. Nobody tell them. As for non-terrorists who fit that profile (which would unfortunately include Jesus himself should he come back and try to enter the United States with his real name Yeshua Bin Yosef), get ready to take one for the team.

An African looking person with an exotic sounding name?

Well, fortunately for Barack Obama, he does not work for say Microsoft or Motorola, instead of the White House, otherwise he'd be spending his days at airports.

But never mind the absurdity in a system that is unfriendly to people who look like our president and Jesus, here's the real problem with racial profiling: it is ineffective. There are two main reasons for that, the first is scientific as concluded by what few studies on racial profiling have taken place.

Profiling Targets the Last Terrorist

The second is logical:

Think about it, the purpose of security checkpoints is to prevent future terror attacks, not past ones. If it is future ones, then should we *limit* ourselves to what *did* happen or would it make more sense to address the possibilities of what *could* happen?

Racial profiling is an elusive game, and [terrorist network] Al Qaeda can always racially profile too. This is not a probability game, one improbable situation is enough to do the damage we hope to prevent.

Do we really want a system where we are always one step behind?

Say we do go for the bearded brown guy, Al Qaeda will send a clean-shaven black one next. Oh wait, they already did; in fact, one that looks like your average all-state American high school athlete. Will that now be the next profile to look out for?

And when we've flagged all Middle-Eastern and Black men with exotic names, they are going to send a white British guy with an Anglo name like Richard Reid. Oh wait, they already did that. And after they send a Russian recruit and a Chinese one and we start profiling all men of all races, they'll recruit a woman. Oh wait, there were two cases of women blowing up Russian airliners in 2004.

The Only True Security

At this rate, the only profile that won't be racially profiled is that Scandinavian grandmother everyone keeps talking about.

Of course, after billions are spent and humanity inconvenienced to no avail, we could always go back to actually acting upon hard intelligence and actually detecting bomb material at airports.

Or, we could do that now.

Analyze the essay:

1. Rehab is an American Muslim who has precisely the kind of name he says officials would likely profile at an airport. How do you think his identity has informed his opinion on the issue of racial profiling? Does the fact that he is an American Muslim make you more likely to agree with his argument? Less likely? Why? Explain your reasoning and use examples from the texts you have read.

2. Rehab suggests that terror organizations are flexible and always evolving and predicts they will simply start to send terrorists who defy racial profiles. In other words, if they know authorities are looking for men, they will send a woman; if they know authorities are screening people who are Arab, they will send someone who is white. Do you agree with him that this is likely how a terrorist organization would respond to racial profiling as a security measure? Do you think this is a good reason to reject racial profiling measures? Why or why not?

Racial Profiling Helps Prevent Illegal Immigration

Heather Mac Donald

In the following essay, Heather Mac Donald discusses a controversial piece of legislation adopted by the state of Arizona in 2010. The law, known as SB 1070, aims to curb illegal immigration and is the toughest such law in the country. It allows police to detain people who fail to carry their immigration papers and to stop anyone suspected of being in the country illegally. Mac Donald argues that there is nothing wrong with this law—it is a valid way of catching people who are not supposed to be here and a good way to discourage more from coming illegally. By definition, she says, illegal immigrants—largely from Mexico, in the case of Arizona—will have a specific appearance, nationality, and ethnicity that makes them identifiable to law enforcement. Police cannot deny this reality when they are looking for illegal immigrants, says Mac Donald, nor should they. She concludes that SB 1070 is a fair and reasonable way to enforce the country's laws that say foreigners are not supposed to be in the country illegally.

Mac Donald is a conservative political columnist and contributing editor to *City Journal*, a publication of the Manhattan Institute, a public policy research organization, where she is a fellow.

As each day passes without any abatement in the increasingly surreal hysteria over the Arizona immigration law, the ground for that opposition becomes ever clearer: The real problem with the Arizona law is that it threatens to make immigration enforcement a reality. Every other argument against it is a smoke screen.

The two main lines of attack against SB 1070—that it is preempted by federal immigration laws and that it will lead to racial profiling—make sense only if you believe that we should not be enforcing our immigration laws.

Immigration Laws Should Be Enforced

Putting state resources behind immigration enforcement interferes with federal enforcement only if it is federal policy not to enforce the immigration laws. Without question, more people will be picked up in Arizona for being in the country illegally with SB 1070 than would have been picked up without SB 1070. Arizona has only several hundred ICE [Immigration and Customs Enforcement] agents, and they are overmatched by the estimated 560,000 illegal aliens in the state. Authorizing the state's 15,000 police officers and deputies to inquire into suspected illegal aliens' immigration status during lawful stops acts as a significant force multiplier for ICE.

That is SB 1070's only effect. Opponents of SB 1070 can argue that a state's detection of illegal aliens conflicts with federal policy only if it is federal policy that those illegal aliens never be subjected to the immigration laws in the first place. Everything that the [Barack] Obama administration has said regarding SB 1070, as well as its implementation of the 287(g) and Secure Communities programs, suggests that such lax enforcement is in fact its de facto stance on immigration.

The Law Does Not Mandate Profiling

President Obama reiterated the racial-profiling trope in his meeting [in May 2010] with Mexico's president, Felipe

Arizona governor Jan Brewer signs the controversial SB 1070 immigration bill into law on April 23, 2010. Brewer says the law will protect Arizona citizens from racial profiling, but the US Justice Department disagrees and has taken the state to court.

Calderón: "We're examining any implications, especially for civil rights, because in the United States of America, no law-abiding person, be they an American citizen, a legal immigrant, or a visitor or tourist from Mexico, should ever be subject to suspicion simply because of what they look like."

The Arizona legislature agrees. SB 1070 states that a law-enforcement officer may make an inquiry regarding someone's immigration status only if he has reasonable suspicion—a longstanding legal concept requiring defensible objective facts—for thinking that the person may be in the country illegally, and only if the officer has stopped or detained that person as part of an independent and lawful police investigation. What someone "looks like" is not a sufficient basis for reasonable suspicion under the law, *pace* Obama. The most likely trigger for an officer's immigration inquiry under SB 1070 will be driving without a license or not possessing another form of valid government identification during a lawful stop, having no credible explanation for the lack of identification, and giving answers that suggest possible illegal status. If someone presents a valid ID, any possibility of reasonable suspicion arising is gone.

> ## Laws That Require Immigrants to Carry Papers Make Sense
>
> Most of us have no qualms about keeping a photocopy of our proof of insurance in our glove compartment, or about being asked for our driver's license or registration. Yet somehow, the notion that immigrants should keep a photocopy of their passport, green card, birth certificate, or visa in their glove compartments makes us Nazi Germany. The truth is that many developed countries around the world require citizens to have some form of a national I.D.
>
> David Seminara, "What Does America's 48th State Have in Common with Nazi Germany, the Soviet Union, and Apartheid-Era South Africa?," Center for Immigration Studies, April 26, 2010. www.cis .org/seminara/arizona-misinformation.

Rendering the Law Nonsensical

But let's be honest: National origin is an inevitable part of immigration enforcement. Foreign alienage is a prerequisite to being an illegal alien; to say that national origin may not be a factor in assessing whether someone may be in the country illegally is to render immigration law nonsensical. If foreign alienage were not a valid consideration regarding border control, incoming passengers

Americans Support Arizona Legislation That Cracks Down on Illegal Immigration

A 2010 poll asked Americans whether they thought SB 1070, an Arizona law designed to crack down on illegal immigration, might lead to racial profiling. The majority said they supported the law.

Question: "A new law in Arizona would give police the power to ask people they've stopped to verify their residency status. Supporters say this will help crack down on illegal immigration. Opponents say it could violate civil rights and lead to racial profiling. On balance, do you support or oppose this law?"

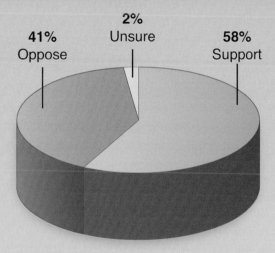

41% Oppose

2% Unsure

58% Support

Taken from: ABC News/*Washington Post* poll, June 3–6, 2010.

on international flights could not be separated into U.S. citizens and non-U.S. citizens for customs clearance.

Yet the illegal-alien lobby, in its nuclear assault on the Arizona law, has managed to discredit notice of foreign birth as a factor in immigration enforcement and to fold foreign alienage into the utterly lethal category of "racial profiling." The original version of SB 1070 said that a "law enforcement official . . . may not solely consider . . . national origin in implementing the requirements of this subsection except to the extent permitted by the United States or Arizona

Arizona citizens rally in support of SB 1070.

Constitution." In the uproar that followed passage of the law, Arizona legislators took out "solely." It is not clear how this change affects legislative intent or the impact of the law. The Supreme Court has allowed border-patrol agents to use apparent foreign birth as one factor in the initial decision to make a car stop near the border. Lower courts have applied that ruling in cases challenging car stops far from the border as well, allowing apparent foreign alienage to count as one part of reasonable suspicion in initiating a stop, so long as the stop was based on other specific, articulable facts as well. SB 1070 is narrower than those rulings, since it applies only to the development of reasonable suspicion after a stop has already been made. To argue, as the illegal-alien lobby is currently doing, that a local law-enforcement officer may not consider apparent foreign origin in deciding whether to ask someone about his immigration status is tantamount to shutting down immigration enforcement entirely.

Who the Illegal Immigrants Are

And let's be honest about another fact as well: There is a greater chance that a legal-alien Hispanic in Arizona driving without his license could have a question asked of him regarding his immigration status during a stop than a native-born Anglo driving without his license. According to the illegal-alien lobby, that possibility renders the law unconstitutional and a fundamental assault on human rights. But the police may question someone based on reasonable suspicion even if, after the fact, it turns out that the person is not breaking the law. And the minimal intrusion on lawful Hispanics from being asked about their immigration status must be balanced against the massive effects on Arizona from the absence of immigration enforcement.

Again, if the possibility that a lawfully resident alien or person of ethnic ancestry may be asked a question about his status is unconstitutional, then we can't have any immigration enforcement at all. Given the breakdown in border control, immigration enforcement will always have a disparate impact on members of the national origin groups who form the greatest portion of illegal aliens. That is not "racial profiling," it's common sense, something that is in short supply surrounding the Arizona law.

Analyze the essay:

1. Mac Donald argues that it is disingenuous to pretend that illegal immigrants, as a group, do not share certain ethnic or national characteristics. Do you agree with her? Should police, when looking for illegal immigrants, assume they will look a certain way? Why or why not?

2. Heather Mac Donald and Mary Bauer, author of the following essay, disagree on whether using racial profiling can or should be used to prevent illegal immigration. After reading both essays, with which author do you agree on this topic? Why? List at least one piece of evidence that convinced you.

Racial Profiling Violates Immigrants' Constitutional Rights

Mary Bauer

Mary Bauer is the legal director at the Southern Poverty Law Center, a nonprofit civil rights organization. In the following essay she argues that allowing police to detain and arrest people they suspect are in the country illegally is unfair, violates the Constitution, and encourages racism and racial profiling. Bauer explains that SB 1070—a 2010 Arizona law that made it legal for police who have stopped someone for a legal infraction to inquire into that person's citizenship status—threatens to violate the civil rights of American citizens and legal immigrants. She also predicts it will hamper police efforts, both by making people of certain communities unwilling to cooperate with the police and by making those same people a target of others. In her opinion, laws that encourage or incorporate racial profiling are un-American and unconstitutional. There are better and fairer ways to enforce the nation's immigration laws, she maintains.

Consider the following questions:

1. What percentage of Arizona's population is Latino, according to Bauer?
2. What is the Pioneer Fund as described by the author?
3. What effect does Bauer say SB 1070 will have on the Latino community's willingness to interact with law enforcement?

Mary Bauer, "Arizona Immigration Law Violates Constitution, Guarantees Racial Profiling," Southern Poverty Law Center, April 28, 2010. http://splcenter.org. © 2010 Southern Poverty Law Center. All rights reserved.

Arizona's newly adopted [in 2010] immigration law [SB 1070] is brazenly unconstitutional and will undoubtedly trample upon the civil rights of residents caught in its path. By requiring local law enforcement to arrest a person when there is "reasonable suspicion" that the person is in the country illegally, Arizona lawmakers have created a system that guarantees racial profiling. They also have usurped federal authority by attempting to enforce immigration law. Quite simply, this law is a civil rights disaster and an insult to American values. No one in our country should be required to produce their "papers" on demand to prove their innocence. What kind of country are we becoming?

Erick Ruark, right, director of the Federation of American Immigration Reform (FAIR), testifies before the US Congress on immigration reform.

An Excuse to Target Brown People

When Arizona Governor Jan Brewer was asked what an undocumented immigrant looks like, she responded: "I do not know what an illegal immigrant looks like. I can tell you that I think there are people in Arizona who assume that they know what an illegal immigrant looks like."

We all know what the outcome of all this double-talk will be. People with brown skin—regardless of whether they are U.S. citizens or legal residents—will be forced to prove their legal status to law enforcement officers time and again. One-third of Arizona's population—those who are Latino—will be designated as second-class citizens, making anyone with brown skin a suspect even if their families have called Arizona home for generations.

Racial Profiling Encourages Discrimination

[Requiring people to verify their immigration status when stopped by police] might be justifiable if all Americans—whether it's someone whose ancestors came over on the Mayflower or a Somali immigrant who took the naturalization oath last week—were required to carry citizenship papers, but that's not the case. [Such a] law would create a discriminatory system, effectively requiring hundreds of thousands of non-white . . . residents—people just as American as their white neighbors—to carry papers with them proving their legal status.

"Arizona-Style Immigration Law Would Invite Racial Profiling," *Holland (MI) Sentinel*, March 11, 2010. www.hollandsentinel.com/opinions/x1777799364 /OUR-VIEW-Arizona-style-immigration-law-would -invite-racial-profiling.

The Racism Behind the Law

Given the authors of this law, no one should be surprised about its intended targets. The law was drafted by a lawyer for the legal arm of the Federation for American Immigration Reform (FAIR), whose founder has warned of a "Latin onslaught" and complained about Latinos' alleged low "educability." FAIR has accepted $1.2 million from the Pioneer Fund, a racist foundation that was set up by Nazi sympathizers to fund studies of eugenics, the science of selective breeding to produce a "better" race. The legislation was sponsored by state Senator Russell Pearce, who once e-mailed an anti-Semitic article from the neo-Nazi National Alliance website to supporters.

Making matters worse, lawmakers have allowed citizens to sue local law enforcement agencies that they

believe are not adequately enforcing the new law. One can be sure that FAIR and its proxies are salivating at the prospects.

Making Law Enforcement More Difficult

The law is not only unconstitutional, it's bad public policy and will interfere with effective policing in Arizona's communities. That's why the legislation was opposed by the Arizona Association of Chiefs of Police. As Latinos grow more fearful of law enforcement, they will be more reluctant to report crimes, and witnesses will be less likely to cooperate with police. Criminals will target the Latino community, confident their victims will keep quiet.

Lawmakers in other states are eager to replicate this ill-advised law. Their frustration with current immigration policy is understandable, but this system must be remedied by our Congress, which should enact fair immigration reform. The federal government must craft a policy that repairs our broken immigration system and, at the same time, protects our most cherished values. States that attempt to follow Arizona's example will only succeed in sowing fear, discord and intolerance in our communities while undermining law enforcement and inviting costly constitutional challenges.

Analyze the essay:

1. Part of Bauer's argument hinges on the idea that no one in the United States, a country renowned for its dedication to freedom and justice, should have to produce papers or documents to prove their innocence. Do you agree with her? How, in your opinion, can the United States balance its dedication to freedom and justice with its need to enforce its immigration laws?

2. Bauer argues that SB 1070 is wrong because it will violate the civil rights of American citizens and legal immigrants, who are constitutionally protected from unreasonable searches and detentions. How would you feel if police stopped you and asked to see documentation? Would you resent it? Would you accept it? Why or why not? Explain your reasoning.

The United States Should Racially Profile Muslims

Asra Q. Nomani

In the following essay Asra Q. Nomani argues that the United States should prevent terrorism by racially profiling Muslims. She says that Muslims with ethnic ties to a handful of nations commit or plot the majority of terrorist attacks. Therefore, in her opinion, it makes sense to screen these people when trying to identify potential terrorists. She says that the broader Muslim community deserves to be profiled because they have failed to adequately discourage terrorism among their own people. Nomani argues that profiling need not be discriminatory or violent; it is just a precaution that every person— especially a Muslim American like herself—should be willing to submit to in the quest for safety and security.

Nomani is a women's rights activist and the author of *Standing Alone: An American Woman's Struggle for the Soul of Islam.*

Consider the following questions:

1. Who is Deroy Murdock and how does the author describe him?
2. What five countries does Nomani say most accused terrorism defendants come from?
3. Who are Ramzi Yousef, Khalid Sheikh Mohammad, and Omar Sheikh, as mentioned by the author?

Asra Q. Nomani, "Airport Security: Let's Profile Muslims," *The Daily Beast,* November 29, 2010. http://thedailybeast.com. © 2011 Asra Q. Nomani. All rights reserved.

For all those holiday travelers negotiating the Transportation Security Administration's [TSA's] new cop-a-feel strategy [that is, physically patting down passengers who are deemed to need additional screening], there is a difficult solution we need to consider: racial and religious profiling.

As an American Muslim, I've come to recognize, sadly, that there is one common denominator defining those who've got their eyes trained on U.S. targets: *Many* of them are Muslim—like the Somali-born teenager arrested Friday night for a reported plot to detonate a car bomb at a packed Christmas tree-lighting ceremony in downtown Portland, Oregon.

Profiling Does Not Equal Discrimination

We have to talk about the taboo topic of profiling because terrorism experts are increasingly recognizing that religious ideology makes terrorist organizations and terror-

Pakistani security officials investigate the site of a terrorist car bombing. Pakistan is among the countries that produce the greatest number of terrorists.

ists more likely to commit heinous crimes against civilians, such as blowing an airliner out of the sky. Certainly, it's not an easy or comfortable conversation, but it's one, I believe, we must have. . . .

I realize that in recent years, profiling has become a dirty word, synonymous with prejudice, racism, and bigotry. But while I believe our risk assessment should not end with religion, race and ethnicity, I believe that it should include these important elements, as part of a "triage" strategy that . . . former CIA case officer Robert Baer says airports and airliners already do.

Profiling doesn't have to be about discrimination, persecution, or harassment. As . . . conservative columnist Deroy Murdock put it: "We are not arguing that the TSA should send anyone named Mohammad to be waterboarded [tortured] somewhere between the [airport's] first-class lounge and the Pizza Hut." . . .

The Muslim Community Has Failed

I [have] said, "Profile me. Profile my family," because, in my eyes, we in the Muslim community have failed to police ourselves. . . .

To me, profiling isn't about identity politics but about threat assessment.

According to a terrorism database at the University of Maryland, which documents 60 attacks against airlines and airports between 1970 and 2007, the last year available, suspects in attacks during the 1970s were tied to the Jewish Defense League, the Black Panthers, the Black September, the National Front for the Liberation of Cuba, Jewish Armed Resistance and the Croatian Freedom Fighters, along with a few other groups.

In each of these groups' names was a religious or ethnic dimension. For that time, those were the identities that we needed to assess. Today, the threat has changed, and it is primarily coming from Muslims who embrace [Islamic terrorist network] al Qaeda's radical brand of Islam.

Islamists Commit More Terrorist Acts than Non-Islamists

According to statistics released by the US Department of Justice and cataloged by the Investigative Project on Terrorism, Islamist motivation was detected in a substantial percentage of terror-related convictions between 2001 and 2010. For this reason, some people believe Muslims should be profiled by law enforcement and security officials.

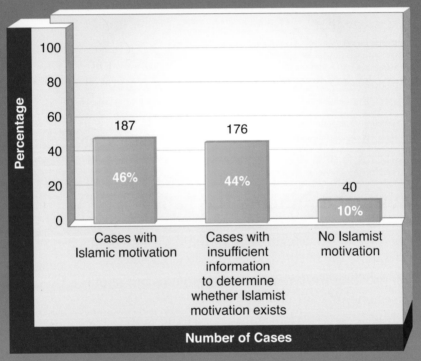

Taken from: "International Terrorism and Terrorism-Related Convictions 9/11/01–3/18/10," Investigative Project on Terrorism, March 9, 2011.

Most Threats Came from One Source

Data in reports released over the past several months from New York University's Center for Security and the Law, the Congressional Research Service, and the Rand Corporation reveal that over the past decade not only are many defendants in terrorism cases Muslim, but they trace their national or ethnic identity back to specific countries.

According to the Rand study "Would-Be Warriors," the national origins or ethnicities [of] most defendants . . . was Pakistan, Somalia, Yemen, Jordan and Egypt, with a handful from the Muslim areas of the Balkans.

To be sure, according to New York University's Center for Security and the Law "Terrorist Trial Report Card," an analysis of terrorism cases prosecuted between 2001 and 2009 reveals that identifying race and ethnicity doesn't mean stereotyping according to country. Among the hundreds of defendants in the study, the largest number held U.S. citizenship. Law enforcement officials familiar with the cases said many of the Americans were ethnically connected to Pakistan, the Palestinian territories, Jordan, Iraq and Egypt. The study, however, didn't look specifically at the ethnicities of the U.S. citizens. According to the study, there were high incidents of cases of passport holders from those countries among the defendants.

Racial Profiling Makes Security Sense

The current threat to passengers and airliners comes almost exclusively from one source, and we all know what it is: young males between about 18 and 35 who practice a fundamentalist strain of the Islamic faith, and generally hail from the Middle East, as well as largely Muslim nations in Africa and South Asia. . . . We are not arguing that the [Transportation Security Administration] should send anyone named Mohammed to be water-boarded [tortured] somewhere between the [airport's] first class lounge and the Pizza Hut. However, if you are a male between about 18 and 35 and are traveling on a Middle Eastern passport or one from a predominantly Muslim country, it might be smart to ask you a few extra questions, carefully peruse your papers, and if things seem unusual we perhaps should take a closer look at your luggage.

Deroy Murdock, "U.S. Airports Should Use Racial and Religious Profiling," Intelligence Squared U.S., Rosenkranz Foundation, November 22, 2010, p. 4. http://intelligencesquaredus.org/wp-content/uploads/airport-profiling-112210.pdf.

The Long History of Muslim Plots

The track record of Muslim plots against airliners and airports is clear, starting with the 1988 bombing of Pan Am 103 over Lockerbie, Scotland. After the first World Trade Center attack in 1993, Ramzi Yousef schemed with his uncle, Khalid Sheikh Mohammed, a Muslim of Pakistani Baluchi ethnicity, to blow up 12 jetliners traveling from Asia to the U.S., intending to kill as many as 4,000 people. The plan fell apart in 1995 after a chemical fire caught the attention of police in the Philippines, but a test run had already killed one passenger seated near a nitroglycerin bomb on a Philippine Airlines flight.

Three years later, [al Qaeda leader] Osama bin Laden threatened to bring down U.S. and Israeli aircrafts through the International Islamic Front for Fighting Against the Jews and Crusaders, warning the attacks would be "pitiless and violent" and announcing that "the war has begun."

"Our response to the barbaric bombardment against Muslims of Afghanistan and Sudan will be ruthless and violent," he said in a statement. "All the Islamic world has mobilized to strike a prominent American or Israeli strategic objective, to blow up their airplanes and to seize them." A declassified CIA memo written in December 1998 warned: "Bin Ladin preparing to hijack U.S. aircraft."

In 1999, we had a "Millennium bomber," targeting Los Angeles International Airport. And, in a case that became very personal to me, on Dec. 24, 1999, a group of Pakistani Muslim militants hijacked an Indian Airlines jet from Kathmandu, Nepal, diverting it to Kandahar, Afghanistan, killing one newlywed passenger. In exchange for the passengers, India released Muslim militants, including a Pakistan-British Muslim militant named Omar Sheikh. Sheikh went on to mastermind the 2002 kidnapping of my friend, *Wall Street Journal* reporter Daniel Pearl, whom Khalid Sheikh Mohammed later confessed to killing.

After the Kathmandu hijacking, we had the 9/11 attacks. And since then, we've had the "Torrance Plotters," the "JFK Airport Plotters," the Glasgow, Scotland, bombers, and the "Transatlantic bombers," all targeting airlines and airports. More recently, there was the attempt by the "underwear bomber," Umar Farouk Abdulmutallab, who last Christmas [2009] attempted to blow up explosives in his underwear—a foiled attack that brought the pat-downs of today. In addition to the Portland plot, most recently, we had the package bomb attempt out of Yemen last month [October 2010].

"A Dangerous Combination"

Victor Asal, a political science professor at State University of New York [SUNY] at Albany, and Karl Rethemeyer, a

professor of public administration and policy at SUNY at Albany, have studied 395 terrorist organizations in operation between 1998 and 2005, and Asal concludes, "What makes terrorist organizations more lethal is religious ideology. When you combine religion and ethnonationalism, you get a dangerous combination."

Asal, the son of a Tunisian father, says there hasn't been enough research done for him to take a stand on racial and religious profiling, but favors "behavioral profiling," which assesses risky behavior like buying one-way tickets with cash and flying without checked baggage.

As attorney R. Spencer MacDonald put it in an article in the *Brigham Young University Journal of Public Law*, we can have "rational profiling."

I know this is an issue of great distress to many people. But I believe that we cannot bury our heads in the sand anymore. We have to choose pragmatism over political correctness, and allow U.S. airports and airlines to do religious and racial profiling.

Since the 1988 bombing of Pan Am Flight 103 over Scotland, airplanes have become a favored target of terrorists.

Analyze the essay:

1. Asra Q. Nomani is a Muslim American. In this essay, not only does she advocate for the racial profiling of Muslim Americans, but she also says, "Profile me. Profile my family." Does it surprise you that a Muslim American would be so supportive of profiling in his or her own community? Why, or why not? Use examples from the texts you have read in your answer.

2. Nomani argues that most terrorists come from Muslim communities. How do you think Yousef Munayyer, author of the following essay, would respond to this claim? Write a few sentences on what you think Munayyer might say in response. Then, state with which author you ultimately agree.

Muslims Should Not Be Profiled

Viewpoint Six

Yousef Munayyer

In the following essay Yousef Munayyer argues that Muslims should not be racially profiled. He argues that focusing on Muslims causes authorities to miss terrorists who come from other ethnic and national groups. Although Muslims commit some terrorist attacks, Munayyer points out that white Christians commit many others. One such white terrorist is Anders Behring Breivik, who in July 2011 killed more than seventy Norwegian citizens in that nation's worst terrorist attack. Munayyer says terrorists like Breivik take advantage of the fact that authorities will not be looking for someone like them and thus slip past security or kill additional people because too few police suspect them. Breivik says that racial profiling encourages a hatred of Muslims that is not only unfair and discriminatory but actually helps motivate attacks like Breivik's. For all of these reasons he concludes that racial profiling makes for poor security.

Munayyer is a Washington, DC–based writer and political analyst. He is the executive director of the Jerusalem Fund for Education and Community Development.

Consider the following questions:

1. How did the media initially respond to the July 2011 terrorist attack in Norway, according to Munayyer?
2. Who, according to the author, looks more like someone who might compete in the Winter Olympics than like a terrorist?
3. What is the "Islamist boogeyman" as described by Munayyer?

ozens of innocents were murdered by a terrorist act in Norway. But not all the casualties were human. Other casualties included some dangerous but commonly-held assumptions about terrorism. Guesses about Islamist involvement came pouring in over the airwaves when news of the bombing broke. These were not seriously questioned by journalists but rather willfully accepted as fact. The [July 22, 2011] bombing in Oslo, the experts said, featured "all the hallmarks" of an al Qaeda attack. Norway, we were told, was on al Qaeda's hit list both because of its NATO [North Atlantic Treaty Organization] involvement in Afghanistan, and because a Norwegian newspaper republished a controversial Islamophobic cartoon originally published in Denmark.

It turned out, of course, that the perpetrator was not an al Qaeda operative but rather a right-wing ethnic Norwegian terrorist [named Anders Behring Breivik] who explicitly targeted what he termed "traitorous" European politicians that advocated less restrictive immigration policies. Breivik's 1500 + page manifesto explains his ideology, which is heavily predicated on maintaining the purity of Europe by defending it from Muslim immigration.

A Deeply Ingrained Bias

Yet even after news reports began to emerge from eyewitnesses who said the attacker was a tall blonde with typical Norwegian looks, the mainstream media was more inclined to believe that some Islamist group was still behind it. In fact, the *New York Times* and other outlets kept the claim of an Islamist connection up on their homepages for hours after it became clear that the culprit was a Norwegian right-winger.

The initial claim of responsibility for the attacks was made on a so-called Jihadi [Muslim "holy warrior"] website by a group that no one had ever heard of. Many in the mainstream media clung to this claim in their reporting, finding it more plausible to believe than the possibility that a Norwegian might have been behind the attacks.

Terrorists Come from All Nations

In reality, domestic terrorism is far more common than transnational terrorism, even in the recent period. From 1998–2005, for example, terror attacks have claimed the lives of 26,445 people, of which only 6,447 were a result of transnational terror (3,000 of those casualties occurred on 9/11).

Has al Qaeda so convinced the West of its ubiquitous power that it is easier for observers to jump to irrational conclusions based on anonymous internet chatter? This seems to be the case.

Norwegian terrorist Anders Behring Breivik killed sixty-nine of his countrymen in a terror attack on July 22, 2011.

This exaggeration, this Islamist boogeyman, contributes directly to the failure to conceptualise and imagine threats like Breivik and his ilk. With the discussions on terrorism in both the public and policy realm overly saturated with analysis on Islam and Islamists, it becomes very easy to miss this right-wing terror threat.

Focusing on Muslims Misses Other Threats

In 2009, the US Department of Homeland Security [DHS] released an important report on the threat of right-wing extremism. The report would later be "withdrawn by the department after criticism from conservatives" and, according to the author of the report, who not surprisingly no longer works at DHS, "the number of analysts assigned to non-Islamic militancy of all kinds was reduced to two from six."

After the report, the US witnessed a dramatic spike in Islamophobia and the growth of the "birther movement" and the Tea Party.[1] The latter is identified by Breivik in his manifesto as "one of the first physical, political manifestations which indicate that there is a great storm coming."

But with the floodgates of hate now opened on innocents in Norway and storm clouds gathering in the United States, will the counter-terrorism discussion continue to ignore this serious threat?

Many Terrorists Have Been Christians

US Congressman Peter King, now chair of the House Homeland Security Committee, is continuing hearings on homegrown terrorism focused specifically on the radicalisation of Muslim Americans. The hearings completely ignore the possibility of another Timothy McVeigh, or Ted Kaczynski, or Lucas John Helder, or Jim Adkisson,

1. The "birther movement" refers to Americans who doubt that President Barack Obama was born in the United States (thus illegitimizing his presidency); the Tea Party is a loosely organized conservative political movement.

or Andrew Joseph Stack, or Jared Lee Loughner—et cetera.

Representative King not only focuses exclusively on Muslims in America, he has also advocated racial profiling as part of the counter-terrorism effort. Just as Breivik destroyed assumptions about terrorism while committing these heinous acts, he also shattered the myth of effective racial profiling. Breivik looks more like someone you might see hopping into a bobsled at the Winter Olympics, not the type you expect to see getting a thorough screening at the airport.

There is irony, perhaps, in the fact that Breivik wasn't only not working for al Qaeda, as many speculators thought might be the case when news of the bombing broke, but he was also virulently anti-Muslim and pro-Israel.

In his manifesto he states "let us fight together with Israel, with our Zionist brothers against all anti-Zionists" and speaks of "assisting Israel in deporting all Muslim Syrians (also referred to as 'Palestinians') from the Gaza strip, the West bank and Jerusalem" and "demolish[ing] the abomination known as the Al Aqsa mosque and the Dome of the Rock in Jerusalem and rebuild the Temple of Salomon [sic]".

The Islamist Boogeyman

Breivik's hatred of Muslims was central to his ideology, and he based much of his thinking and writing on prominent American Islamophobes. Characters like [Jihad Watch founder] Robert Spencer, whom Breivik identifies as a leading "intellectual", along with others like Pamela Geller and outted fake Walid Shoebat, have been at the epicenter of the Islamophobic industry in the United States. They were some of the main leaders of the

---

Terrorists Come in All Colors

Timothy McVeigh killed more than 160 people when he set off bombs in Oklahoma City in 1995. He looked like the all-American boy. He paid for his crimes, but no one ever becomes uncomfortable in airports when they see people who look like McVeigh. [Norwegian terrorist Anders Behring] Breivik will likely be written off as an anomaly— some right-wing nut, who is probably mentally ill . . . and not part of some wider conspiracy to commit mass murder on innocent people. Meanwhile, people with olive-to-dark brown complexions, beards and (especially) turbans, will continue to be watched with extreme suspicion and fear.

Palash R. Ghosh, "Will Blonde-Haired, Blue-Eyed White Men Now Be Racially Profiled?," *International Business Times*, July 25, 2011. www.ibtimes.com /articles/186297/20110725/oslo-norway-terrorism -murder-profiling-racial-anders-behring-breivik.htm.

anti-Park 51 movement[2] prior to the last congressional elections. They are also supporters of the birther movement, which believes that President [Barack] Obama is secretly a Muslim. Breivik quotes extensively from the writings of these fear-peddlers, and has clearly been influenced by their arguments.

While these writers and bloggers are now frantically trying to distance themselves from Breivik by claiming that they never advocated violence, they contributed to the horrors that took place in Norway by dehumanising an entire religion and its followers and advancing a fear-inspiring, cataclysmic us-versus-them mentality. Sure, Breivik may have acted alone in pulling a trigger, but the Islamophobic industry gladly drew the bullseye.

Short-Sighted Assumptions

The only thing worse than failing to anticipate right-wing terrorists like Breivik because of short-sighted assumptions is failing to do so again, now that we've witnessed what they are capable of. Western nations must take this opportunity to reflect on the attacks in Norway and ask what is being done to prevent this from happening again.

First, there needs to be a serious rethinking about the Islamist boogeyman and a reevaluation of the share of security and intelligence resources dedicated exclusively to it.

Second, Breivik's attacks should put to rest the idea that complex networks or cells are necessary to pull off massive and devastating attacks.

Third, Breivik's ethnic background and the fact that he knew it would help him "escape the scrutiny often reserved for young men of Arab descent" should put to rest any discussion about racial profiling as an effective or efficient security measure.

2. People opposed to the building of an Islamic cultural center near the site of the 9/11 terrorist attacks in New York City.

Muslim Terrorists Are in the Minority

Data compiled by the Muslim Public Affairs Council shows that between December 2001 and May 2011, Muslim extremists committed a minority of terrorist attacks against or in the United States. Anti-government extremists accounted for the most attacks.

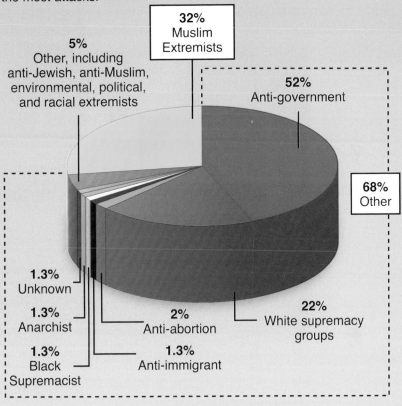

5%
Other, including anti-Jewish, anti-Muslim, environmental, political, and racial extremists

32%
Muslim Extremists

52%
Anti-government

68%
Other

1.3%
Unknown

1.3%
Anarchist

2%
Anti-abortion

22%
White supremacy groups

1.3%
Black Supremacist

1.3%
Anti-immigrant

Taken from: J. Beutel, "Data on Post–9/11 Terrorism in the United States," Muslim Public Affairs Council, June 2011.

Fourth, serious attention must be paid to the radicalisers on the right and the Islamophobes who preach a dichotomous worldview. Explicit calls to violence are clearly not necessary to inspire violence against civilians, and thus right-wing chat forums should receive every

Republican congressman Peter King chairs a committee on domestic terrorism. His committee has been criticized for focusing on Muslims as terrorists, and downplaying the threat from white supremacists and right-wing militia groups.

bit as much scrutiny from terror analysts as so-called jihadi web sites.

Islamophobia Hurts Everyone

The lives of the victims of the tragedy in Norway are lost forever, but we mustn't let their blood be spilt in vain. Instead, we must adjust our assumptions and policies about terrorism and Islamophobia at this critical moment. Breivik wanted to send a "wake-up" call. Let's make sure we're never asleep when Islamophobia or right-wing terrorism tries to shake our societies again.

Analyze the essay:

1. To make his argument, the author references Timothy McVeigh, Ted Kaczynski, Lucas John Helder, Jim Adkisson, Andrew Joseph Stack, and Jared Lee Loughner. Using the resources available in your classroom and school or local library, research each of these people. Write two to three sentences on each. In what way does your research inform your opinion about racial profiling? Explain your answer given what you have learned.

2. Yousef Munayyer and Asra Q. Nomani, the author of the previous essay, disagree on whether it is appropriate to racially profile Muslims. After reading both of their essays, select which author you thought made the better argument. Which points did you find particularly persuasive, and why? What pieces of evidence did you find particularly convincing, and why? Discuss at least one point and one piece of evidence in your answer.

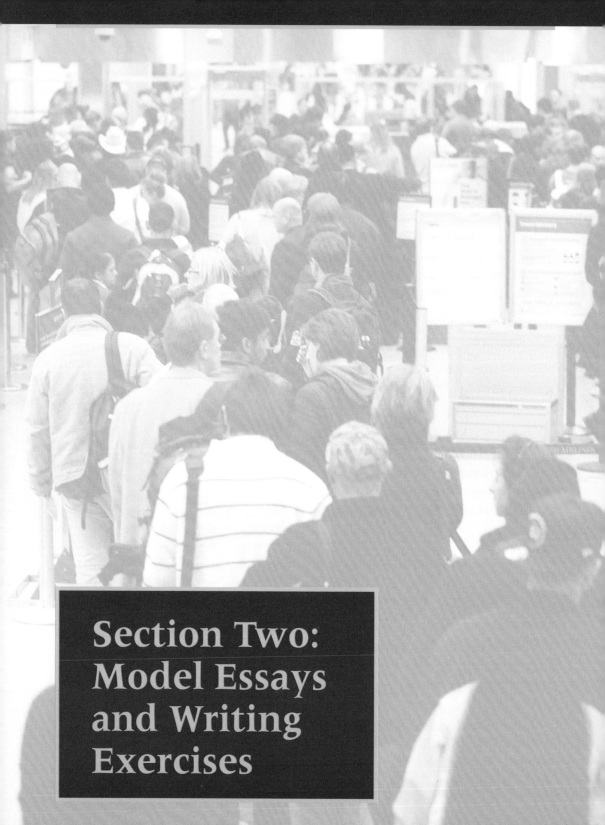

Section Two:
Model Essays
and Writing
Exercises

The Five-Paragraph Essay

An *essay* is a short piece of writing that discusses or analyzes one topic. The five-paragraph essay is a form commonly used in school assignments and tests. Every five-paragraph essay begins with an *introduction,* ends with a *conclusion,* and features three *supporting paragraphs* in the middle.

The Thesis Statement. The introduction includes the essay's thesis statement. The thesis statement presents the argument or point the author is trying to make about the topic. The essays in this book all have different thesis statements because they are making different arguments about racial profiling.

The thesis statement should clearly tell the reader what the essay will be about. A focused thesis statement helps determine what will be in the essay; the subsequent paragraphs are spent developing and supporting its argument.

The Introduction. In addition to presenting the thesis statement, a well-written introductory paragraph captures the attention of the reader and explains why the topic being explored is important. It may provide the reader with background information on the subject matter or feature an anecdote that illustrates a point relevant to the topic. It could also present startling information that clarifies the point of the essay or put forth a contradictory position that the essay will refute. Further techniques for writing an introduction are found later in this section.

The Supporting Paragraphs. The introduction is then followed by three (or more) supporting paragraphs. These are the main body of the essay. Each paragraph presents and develops a *subtopic* that supports the essay's thesis statement. Each subtopic is spearheaded by a *topic sentence* and supported by its own facts, details, and examples. The writer can use various kinds of supporting material and details to back up the topic of each supporting paragraph. These may include statistics, quotations from people with special knowledge or expertise, historic facts, and anecdotes. A rule of writing is that specific and concrete examples are more convincing than vague, general, or unsupported assertions.

The Conclusion. The conclusion is the paragraph that closes the essay. Its function is to summarize or reiterate the main idea of the essay. It may recall an idea from the introduction or briefly examine the larger implications of the thesis. Because the conclusion is also the last chance a writer has to make an impression on the reader, it is important that it not simply repeat what has been presented elsewhere in the essay but close it in a clear, final, and memorable way.

Although the order of the essay's component paragraphs is important, they do not have to be written in the order presented here. Some writers like to decide on a thesis and write the introduction paragraph first. Other writers like to focus first on the body of the essay, and write the introduction and conclusion later.

Pitfalls to Avoid

When writing essays about controversial issues such as racial profiling, it is important to remember that disputes over the material are common precisely because there are many different perspectives. Remember to state your arguments in careful and measured terms. Evaluate your topic fairly—avoid overstating negative qualities of one perspective or understating positive qualities of another. Use examples, facts, and details to support any assertions you make.

The Expository Essay

The previous section of this book provided you with samples of writings on racial profiling. All made arguments or advocated a particular position about racial profiling and related topics. All included elements of *expository* writing as well. The purpose of expository writing is to inform the reader about a particular subject matter. Sometimes a writer will use exposition to simply communicate knowledge; at other times, he or she will use exposition to convince a reader of a particular point of view.

Types of Expository Writing

There are several different types of expository writing. Examples of these types can be found in the viewpoints in the preceding chapter. The list below provides some ideas on how exposition could be organized and presented. Each type of writing could be used separately or in combination in five-paragraph essays.

Definition. *Definition* refers to simply telling what something is. Definitions can be encompassed in a sentence or paragraph. At other times, definitions may take a paragraph or more. The act of defining some topics—especially abstract concepts—can sometimes serve as the focus of entire essays.

Classification. A classification essay describes and clarifies relationships between things by placing them in different categories, based on their similarities and differences. This can be a good way of organizing and presenting information.

Process. A process essay looks at how something is done. The writer presents events or steps in a chronologically or logically ordered sequence of steps. Process writing can either inform the reader of a past event or process by which something was made, or instruct the reader on how to do something.

Illustration. Illustration is one of the simplest and most common patterns of expository writing. Simply put, it explains by giving specific and concrete examples. It is an effective technique for making one's writing both more interesting and more intelligible. Model Essay Two offers an example of illustration. The writer offers the example of Lena Reppert to illustrate why she believes random screening is a less effective security measure than profiling.

Problem/Solution. Problem/solution refers to when the author raises a problem or a question, and then uses the rest of the paragraph or essay to answer the question or provide possible resolutions to the problem. It can be an effective way of drawing in the reader while imparting information to him/her. Many of the viewpoints in Section One of this book used problem/solution. Ensuring the security of Americans or curbing illegal immigration are the problems; whether racial profiling offers a solution to these problems, however, is debated.

Words and Phrases Common to Expository Essays

accordingly	it is important to understand
because	it makes sense to
clearly	it seems as though
consequently	it then follows that
evidently	moreover
first . . . second . . . third	next
for example	since
for this reason	subsequently
from this perspective	therefore
furthermore	this is why
however	thus
indeed	

"Driving While Black" Persists

Editor's Notes The following five-paragraph essay uses definition as an organizing principle. A definition essay describes, defines, or clarifies terms, relationships, objects, concepts, positions, or procedures. You can read more about definition essays (and other types of expository essays) in Preface B of this section.

The following essay uses definition to describe the phenomenon of "driving while black," a catch phrase that describes the way in which African Americans have been disproportionately singled out by police and other law enforcement because of their race. It explains that although the racial profiling of African Americans has been overshadowed in recent years by debates about the profiling of Muslims, it is still an issue for the black community.

The notes in the margin point out key features of the essay and help you understand how it is organized. Also note that all sources are cited using Modern Language Association (MLA) style.* For more information on how to cite your sources see Appendix C. In addition, consider the following:

1. How does the introduction engage the reader's attention?
2. What pieces of supporting evidence are used to back up the essay's points and arguments?
3. What purpose do the essay's quotes serve?
4. How does the author transition from one idea to another?
5. How is definition featured in the essay?

■ Refers to thesis and topic sentences

■ Refers to supporting details

---

* Editor's Note: In applying MLA style guidelines in this book, the following simplifications have been made: Parenthetical text citations are confined to direct quotations only; electronic source documentation in the Works Cited list omits date of access, page ranges, and some detailed facts of publication.

Paragraph 1

Racial profiling—when law enforcement uses a person's appearance as a basis for suspecting them of wrongdoing—has been an issue for decades. In recent years the targets of and debates about racial profiling have come to center on Arab and Muslim men (who are sometimes suspected of plotting terrorism) and Hispanic people (who are sometimes suspected of having entered the United States illegally). But African Americans have long been victims of racial profiling and continue to be disproportionately singled out by police on the road, in stores, and even in their own homes.

Paragraph 2

The issue of racial profiling rose to prominence in the 1990s, as stories increasingly emerged of law enforcement's tendency to single out African Americans. According to Samuel R. Gross, a professor at the University of Michigan Law School, although the practice of racial profiling had been around for decades, the terms "racial profiling" and "driving while black" were first introduced on a large scale in the early 1990s. "In 1988 racial profiling—the term, not the practice—was unknown," says Gross. "By 2000, twelve years later, everyone, from [President] George Bush to [civil rights activist] Jesse Jackson, agreed that racial profiling is anathema [forbidden]."

Paragraph 3

Gross traces one of the first mainstream uses of the phrase "driving while black" to a *New York Times* story printed in May 1990. In April of that year, a white police officer killed a black teenager named Phillip Pannell in Teaneck, New Jersey. The boy was unarmed and was fatally shot as he ran from police, who had been called to the area to investigate a noise complaint. The case inflamed racial tensions and skyrocketed the issue of racial profiling to the national stage. In covering the story, the *Times* quoted a black teenager who lived in Teaneck as saying, "We get arrested for D.W.B.—you know, driving while black." (Qtd. in Golden, B1) Though the phrase had long been used informally, this was one of the first times it was mentioned in a major print publication. A play on the phrase "driving while intoxicated," the implication is that blackness in itself is a crime, one that gives law enforcement the excuse to pull over African American drivers and question, search, or otherwise harass them.

Paragraph 4

In the twenty-first century, the profiling of other groups has overshadowed the racial profiling of African Americans. After the September 11, 2001, terrorist attacks, in which nineteen Middle Eastern men hijacked commercial airliners and flew them into targets around the United States, killing nearly three thousand civilians, Arab and Muslim men became high-profile targets of racial profiling. In a nod to the concept of "driving while black," the profiling of such men by airport security has been dubbed "flying while Arab," and there have been several much-publicized cases in which innocent people have been removed from aircraft or inordinately scrutinized by security simply because of their ethnicity, clothing, or personal appearance. Likewise, in 2010, controversial legislation that allowed Arizona law enforcement to profile people suspected of being in the country illegally spawned the phrase "walking while Latino."

This is the topic sentence of Paragraph 4. It explores a different facet of the essay's thesis than the other paragraphs.

Likewise and although are transitional words. They keep the sentences linked together and the ideas moving.

Paragraph 5

Although these two groups occupy much of the focus and debate about contemporary racial profiling, it is still an issue for the black community. "The experience of being mistaken for a criminal is almost a rite of passage for African-American men," wrote columnist Brent Staples in 2009, the same year that African American scholar and Harvard professor Henry Louis Gates Jr. was arrested in his own home after police mistook him for a burglar. As Gates said, "Security guards shadow us in stores. Troopers pull us over for the crime of 'driving while black.' Nighttime pedestrians cower by us on the streets." That same year, the *Atlantic* reported on a 2008 study of traffic stops in Illinois. The study found that African American drivers were three times as likely to be the subject of a search as white drivers. Moreover, when vehicles were searched, whites were more often found to be hiding contraband. "Police found contraband 24.37 percent of the time when a white agreed to a search, but just 15.14 percent of the time with a minority driver," reported James Warren, who said that although some of the data from the study was open to interpretation, "it's clear that African-American . . . drivers are in fact being stopped more than one would expect based on their overall representation in the driving population." It seems that "driving while black" is still a problem in the United States, even though it gets less attention than it did in the past.

Works Cited

Golden, Tim. "Residents and Police Share Lingering Doubts in Teaneck." *New York Times* 21 May 1990, p. B1. http://www.nytimes.com/1990/05/21/nyregion/residents-and-police-share-lingering-doubts-in-teaneck.html?pagewanted = all&src = pm.

Gross, Samuel R. *The Rhetoric of Racial Profiling.* Public Law and Legal Theory Working pa. no. 66, University of Michigan Law School, October 2006.

Staples, Brent. "Even Now, There's Risk in 'Driving While Black.'" *New York Times* 14 June 2009, p. A20. http://www.nytimes.com/2009/06/15/opinion/15mon4.html.

Warren, James. "Driving While Black." *Atlantic* July 2009. http://www.theatlantic.com/magazine/archive/2009/07/driving-while-black/7625/.

Exercise 1A: Create an Outline from an Existing Essay

It often helps to create an outline of the five-paragraph essay before you write it. The outline can help you organize the information, arguments, and evidence you have gathered during your research.

For this exercise, create an outline that could have been used to write "Driving While Black" Persists. This "reverse engineering" exercise is meant to help familiarize you with how outlines can help classify and arrange information.

To do this you will need to
1. articulate the essay's thesis,
2. pinpoint important pieces of evidence,
3. flag quotes that support the essay's ideas, and
4. identify key points that support the argument.

Part of the outline has already been started to give you an idea of the assignment.

Outline

I. Paragraph 1

Write the essay's thesis: Although the racial profiling of African Americans has been overshadowed by the profiling of other groups, African Americans continue to be disproportionately singled out by police on the road, in stores, and even in their own homes.

II. Paragraph 2
Topic:

Supporting Detail i. The terms "racial profiling" and "driving while black" were first introduced on a large scale in the early 1990s.

Supporting Detail ii. Quote from Samuel R. Gross.

III. Paragraph 3
Topic: One of the first mainstream uses of the phrase "driving while black" occurred in a *New York Times* story printed in May 1990.

Supporting Detail i.

Supporting Detail ii.

IV. Paragraph 4
Topic: In the twenty-first century, the profiling of other groups has overshadowed the racial profiling of African Americans.

Supporting Detail i.

Supporting Detail ii.

V. Paragraph 5
Write the essay's conclusion:

We Know Who Wants to Attack Us—So Let's Profile Them

Editor's Notes Problem/solution refers to when the author raises a problem or a question, then uses the rest of the paragraph or essay to answer the question or provide possible resolutions to the problem. The following sample essay uses problem/solution to argue a position. The problem it puts forth is that there is a limited amount of money and time that can be devoted to screening millions of airline passengers. A solution to this problem, says the author, is to use racial profiling to hone in on the people who are most likely to be a threat. The author then uses the essay's supporting paragraphs to describe each of the ways in which racial profiling offers solutions to the problem posed.

Unlike the first model essay, this expository essay is also persuasive, meaning that the author wants to persuade you to agree with her point of view. As you read, keep track of the notes in the margins. They will help you analyze how the essay is organized and how it is written.

▉ Refers to thesis and topic sentences

▉ Refers to supporting details

Paragraph 1

In June 2011, security agents detained Lena Reppert for additional screening before she boarded a flight from Florida to Michigan. Reppert was what some might call the last person in the world to arouse suspicion of terrorism. Ninety-five-years old and confined to a wheelchair, Reppert was on her way to see family members one last time before she died from cancer. Not satisfied by the invasive pat down they gave her, agents made her remove an adult diaper she was wearing so they could be sure the woman was not smuggling explosives or weapons in it. Humiliating our most vulnerable citizens because they might be killers-in-waiting is not only immoral and indecent, but a waste of scant security resources.

Look at Exercise 3A on introductions. What type of introduction is this? Does it grab your attention?

This is the essay's thesis statement. It gets to the heart of the author's argument.

67

According to the Transportation Security Administration, about 1.2 million people fly in the United States each day, on approximately twenty-eight thousand domestic flights. It is impossible to screen each one of these individuals thoroughly: it would take too much money to employ that many screeners, and it would also be impossible to get anyone to their gate on time. As Deroy Murdock, columnist and media fellow at the Hoover Institution, has put it, "In a world of limited time, personnel, and money, we have no choice but to focus on those people who threaten to destroy aircraft and the flying public who ride within them."

Paragraph 3

To do this, we should not treat everyone as equal suspects: this is never the way police approach quality detective work. "If you set up a sobriety checkpoint, if you're a police department, you most likely would put it somewhere near bars, not close to churches," argues Murdock. "Similarly, if a wave of bank robberies were committed by a black man between ages 45 and 50, and if he were just under six feet tall, and lived in Manhattan's East Village [a profile Murdock fits], I would not be shocked if the police stopped me and asked me a few questions." Murdock's point is that law enforcement officers need to hone in on the people most likely to be perpetrators. Casting a wide net is too expensive and time-consuming and will not yield the people who pose a threat.

Paragraph 4

Because of its efficiency and effectiveness, profiling is used by a country well known for its experience with terrorism: Israel. Indeed, Israeli security agents dispense with political correctness and niceties and make it their priority to catch the people who are Israel's stated enemies. "Our system, the envy of many worldwide . . . , is often disparaged as 'racial profiling,' but it is what allows the great majority of passengers to be waved through after a quick conversation, and with considerably less inconvenience, humiliation and intrusion than frequently encountered

---

What is the topic sentence of Paragraph 2? Look for a sentence that tells generally what the paragraph's main point is.

Why do you think the author has included Deroy Murdock's job title?

This is the topic sentence of Paragraph 3. Without reading the rest of the paragraph, take a guess at what the paragraph will be about.

This quote was taken from the quote box that accompanies Viewpoint One. When you see particularly striking quotes, save them to use to support points in your essays.

in American airports," write the editors at the *Jerusalem Post*. "It also allows security personnel to focus on those who most arouse suspicion. Terror-prevention efforts are thereby rendered both more efficient and effective," they add. Despite numerous enemies around the world, Israel has one of the most impressive airport security records, in large part due to its willingness to profile.

Paragraph 5

There is no need to screen all passengers equally; we know who wants to attack us. Their names are Umar Farouk AbdulMutallab, who tried to blow up a Detroit-bound plan with explosives hidden in his underwear; Najibullah Zazi, who sought to blow up the New York City subway; and Nidal Hasan, who killed twelve and wounded thirty-one in his November 2009 shooting spree at Fort Hood. Our enemies are not Alaska representative Sharon Cissna, a sixty-nine-year old breast cancer survivor who in February 2011 refused to let officials pat down her mastectomy scars; or Jean Weber, Lena Reppert's daughter, who was subjected to additional security when she broke down in tears upon seeing her sick, frail, ninety-five-year-old mother's undergarments removed by security agents. Using profiling is neither discriminatory nor unfair. It is the common sense solution to a problem that threatens to drain us of both our dignity and our resources. Let's stop pretending that the Lena Repperts of the world pose the same threat level as do the AbdulMutallabs, the Zazis, and the Hasans.

Note how the author returns to ideas introduced in Paragraph 1. See Exercise 2A for more on introductions and conclusions.

Works Cited

Murdock, Deroy. "U.S. Airports Should Use Racial and Religious Profiling." Intelligence Squared U.S., Rosenkranz Foundation 22 Nov 2010: 3–5. http://intelligencesquaredus.org/wp-content/uploads/airport-profiling-112210.pdf.

Jerusalem Post. "Keep Our Airports Safe." 9 Mar 2011. http://www.jpost.com/Opinion/Editorials/Article.aspx?id = 211484.

Exercise 2A: Create an Outline from an Existing Essay

As you did for the first model essay in this section, create an outline that could have been used to write "We Know Who Wants to Attack Us—So Let's Profile Them." Be sure to identify the essay's thesis statement, its supporting ideas, and key pieces of evidence that were used.

Exercise 2B: Create an Outline for Your Own Essay

The second model essay discusses a particular aspect of racial profiling. For this exercise, your assignment is to find supporting ideas, choose specific and concrete details, create an outline, and ultimately write a five-paragraph essay making a different point about the topic. Your goal is to use expository techniques to convince your reader.

Part l: Write a thesis statement.

The following thesis statement would be appropriate for an expository essay on why racial profiling makes for lazy police work. The essay would focus on the ways in which relying on racial profiling leads officials to miss people who are outside the profile:

> *Once terrorists know that law enforcement officials have narrowed their search to a particular group of people, they will simply send people who are different.*

Or, see the sample essay topics suggested in Appendix D for more ideas.

Part II: Brainstorm pieces of supporting evidence.

Using information from some of the viewpoints in the previous section and from the information found in Section Three of this book, write down three arguments or pieces of evidence that support the thesis statement you selected. Then, for each of these three arguments, write down supportive facts, examples, and details that support it. These could be:

- statistical information
- personal memories and anecdotes
- quotes from experts, peers, or family members
- observations of people's actions and behaviors
- specific and concrete details

Supporting pieces of evidence for the above sample thesis statement are found in this book and include:

- Points made in Viewpoint Six by Yousef Munayyer about Anders Behring Breivik, a blond Christian who killed more than seventy Norwegians on July 2011 and who would have evaded security officials using racial profiling to catch terrorists.
- Quote from the box that accompanies Viewpoint Two by the editors of the *Baltimore Sun*. They argued that the pat-down of Lena Reppert was necessary: "The TSA can't tell its employees never to give a pat-down to a 95-year-old woman, or a 6-year-old boy, or an adult who doesn't want anyone to touch his 'junk'— to quote a couple of other embarrassing moments for airport screeners. Why? Because as soon as certain classes of people are identified as non-threatening, then terrorists are likely to recruit people who fit that exact profile." For other points, see *Baltimore Sun*, "TSA: Treatment of Elderly Cancer Patient Raises Questions About Airport Screening," June 27, 2011. http://articles.baltimoresun.com/2011-06-27/news /bs-ed-pat-down-20110627_1_pat-down-tsa-cancer -patient.
- Poll data that accompanies Viewpoint Two that shows Americans think personal behavior, travel history, and nationality are more important to pro-file than a person's race or religion.

Part III: Place the information from Part II in outline form.

Part IV: Write the arguments or supporting statements in paragraph form.

By now you have three arguments that support the paragraph's thesis statement, as well as supporting material. Use the outline to write out your three supporting arguments in paragraph form. Make sure each paragraph has a topic sentence that states the paragraph's thesis clearly and broadly. Then, add supporting sentences that express the facts, quotes, details, and examples that support the paragraph's argument. The paragraph may also have a concluding or summary sentence.

Racial Profiling Is Discriminatory, Unfair, and Unconstitutional

Editor's Notes   Yet another way of writing an expository essay is to use illustration. An illustrative expository essay argues its point by giving specific and concrete examples. It is an effective technique for making one's writing both more interesting and more intelligible.

The following model essay uses illustration to argue that racial profiling is discriminatory. It uses the experiences of three different sets of people to illustrate the ways in which racial profiling is unfair, counterproductive, and even unconstitutional.

As you read, consider the questions posed in the margins. Continue to identify thesis statements, supporting details, transitions, and quotations. Examine the introductory and concluding paragraphs to understand how they give shape to the essay. Finally, evaluate the essay's general structure and assess its overall effectiveness.

■ Refers to thesis and topic sentences

■ Refers to supporting details

Paragraph 1

Ever since the September 11, 2001, terrorist attacks, in which Muslim extremists hijacked commercial airliners and killed nearly three thousand people, Muslim Americans have become a target of scrutiny. They are pulled out of line for additional screening in airports; sometimes they are kicked off flights because their presence makes other passengers, even pilots, uneasy. But suspecting all Muslims of terrorism is overt discrimination. Three persons' experiences with and observations on racial profiling illustrate just how unfair, discriminatory, and even unconstitutional this ineffective practice really is.

What is the essay's thesis statement? How did you recognize it?

This is the topic sentence of Paragraph 2. Without reading the rest of the paragraph take a guess at what the paragraph will be about.

What makes the Sayed quote a good choice for this essay? Give two reasons why it works well.

The author is expressing an opinion in this sentence. Opinions are a clue that an essay is persuasive—that is, the author is trying to convince you of a point of view.

Like the quote in the previous paragraph, this type of quote is a primary source because it is from someone who personally experienced profiling. Primary sources enliven essays in many ways.

Paragraph 2

Racial profiling violates Muslim Americans' constitutional rights, as Nafees A. Sayed well knows. A graduate of Harvard University, Sayed now works for the US House of Representatives Judiciary Committee and is also a writer. Sayed wears the Muslim head scarf known as a hijab, and she is pulled aside for additional screening almost every time she flies. "I've been told to take my head scarf off or have my head probed while the passengers in front of me offered pitying smiles as they rushed to their flights," she says. Sayed's experience is not only humiliating and unfair: It violates the Fourth Amendment, which guarantees US citizens protection from unreasonable searches and seizures; it also violates the Fourteenth Amendment, which requires that all US citizens be treated equally under the law. When we violate the rights of our Muslim citizens, we jeopardize everyone's rights and bring dishonor to the US Constitution and to our country as a whole.

Paragraph 3

Sayed is not the only Muslim American who has had her rights violated by profiling. On May 6, 2011, two imams (Muslim clergymen) named Mohamed Zaghloul and Masudur Rahman were removed from a flight heading from Memphis, Tennessee, to Charlotte, North Carolina. Zaghloul and Rahman, who is a professor of Arabic at the University of Memphis, were asked to leave the plane even though they had already cleared all airport security checks and boarded the plane. They were told the pilot had refused to accept them on the flight because they made some of the other passengers uncomfortable. While they were being scrutinized by security, the pilot took off without them, and they missed their flight. "It's racism and bias because of our religion and appearance and because of misinformation about our religion," said Rahman. "If they understood Islam, they wouldn't do this." (Qtd. in *Daily Mail*) Ironically, the clerics were headed to a conference on Islamophobia, which is the suspicion, fear, and hatred of Muslims.

Paragraph 4

Profiling Muslims seems even more wrong when one remembers they too have been victims of terror attacks. In fact, more than sixty Muslim Americans died in the September 11 attacks. Political analyst Rayeed N. Tayeh, who is Muslim, says that Americans need to realize that Muslims have as much at stake as the rest of the country. "When terrorists target America, they target all Americans, Muslims included," reminds Tayeh. It is unfair and even cruel that "Muslims in America have to worry about being victims of terrorism while at the same time worry about being blamed for terrorism," he adds.

> What is the topic sentence of Paragraph 4? How did you recognize it?

Paragraph 5

Racial profiling is largely about fear and bias, but here are some solid facts: With more than 1.2 billion adherents worldwide, nearly one in five people on the planet is a Muslim. *Muhammad* is the most common name on earth. Muslim Americans are citizens with the same constitutional rights and interest in preventing terrorism as everyone else. Singling them out is discriminatory, unfair, unconstitutional, and counterproductive, so let's look elsewhere for solutions to national security problems.

> Note how the essay's conclusion wraps up the topic in a final, memorable way—without repeating the points made in the essay.

Works Cited

"Muslim Religious Leaders Told to Leave U.S. Domestic Flight After Pilot Refuses to Take Off with Them Aboard." *Daily Mail* 7 May 2011. http://www.dailymail.co.uk /news/article-1384592/Muslim-religious-leaders-told -leave-U-S-domestic-flight-pilot-refuses-aboard.html.

Sayed, Nafees A. "Airport Screening for 'Flying While Muslim.'" CNN.com 29 Jan 2010. http://articles.cnn .com/2010-01-29/opinion/syed.muslim.while.flying_1 _profiling-muslim-women-head-scarf?_s = PM:OPINION.

Tayeh, Rayeed N. "I'm Sorry You Are Scared of Me; My Religion Shouldn't Frighten You." *Deseret News* 29 Oct 2010. http://www.deseretnews.com/article/700077154 /Im-sorry-you-are-scared-of-me-my-religion-shouldnt -frighten-you.html.

Exercise 3A: Examining Introductions and Conclusions

Every essay features introductory and concluding paragraphs that are used to frame the main ideas being presented. Along with presenting the essay's thesis statement, well-written introductions should grab the attention of the reader and make clear why the topic being explored is important. The conclusion reiterates the essay's thesis and is also the last chance for the writer to make an impression on the reader. Strong introductions and conclusions can greatly enhance an essay's effect on an audience.

The Introduction

There are several techniques that can be used to craft an introductory paragraph. An essay can start with:

- an anecdote: a brief story that illustrates a point relevant to the topic;
- startling information: facts or statistics that elucidate the point of the essay;
- setting up and knocking down a position: a position or claim believed by proponents of one side of a controversy, followed by statements that challenge that claim;
- historical perspective: an example of the way things used to be that leads into a discussion of how or why things work differently now;
- summary information: general introductory information about the topic that feeds into the essay's thesis statement.

Problem One
Reread the introductory paragraphs of the model essays in this section and of the viewpoints in Section One. Identify which of the techniques described above are used in the viewpoints and model essays. How do they grab the attention of the reader? Are their thesis statements clearly presented?

Problem Two

Write an introduction for the essay you have outlined and partially written in Exercise 2B using one of the techniques described above.

The Conclusion

The conclusion brings the essay to a close by summarizing or returning to its main ideas. Good conclusions, however, go beyond simply repeating these ideas. Strong conclusions explore a topic's broader implications and reiterate why it is important to consider. They may frame the essay by returning to an anecdote featured in the opening paragraph. Or they may close with a quotation or refer back to an event in the essay. In opinionated essays, the conclusion can reiterate which side the essay is taking or ask the reader to reconsider a previously held position on the subject.

Problem Three

Reread the concluding paragraphs of the model essays and of the viewpoints in Section One. Which were most effective in driving their arguments home to the reader? What sorts of techniques did they use to do this? Did they appeal emotionally to the reader, or bookend an idea or event referenced elsewhere in the essay?

Problem Four

Write a conclusion for the essay you have outlined and partially written in Exercise 2B using one of the techniques described above.

Exercise 3B: Using Quotations to Enliven Your Essay

No essay is complete without quotations. Get in the habit of using quotes to support at least some of the ideas in your essays. Quotes do not need to appear in every paragraph but often enough so that the essay contains voices aside from your own. When you write, use quotations to accomplish the following:

- provide expert advice that you are not necessarily in the position to know about;
- cite lively or passionate passages;
- include a particularly well-written point that gets to the heart of the matter;
- supply statistics or facts that have been derived from someone's research;
- deliver anecdotes that illustrate the point you are trying to make;
- express first-person testimony.

Problem One:
Reread the essays presented in the first two sections of this book and find at least one example of each of the above quotation types.

There are a couple of important things to remember when using quotations:

- Note your sources' qualifications and biases. This way your reader can identify the person you have quoted and can put their words in a context.
- Put any quoted material within proper quotation marks. Failing to attribute quotes to their authors constitutes plagiarism, which is when an author takes someone else's words or ideas and presents them as his or her own. Plagiarism is a very serious infraction and must be avoided at all costs.

Write Your Own Five-Paragraph Expository Essay

Using the information in this book, write your own five-paragraph expository essay that deals with an aspect of racial profiling. You can use the resources in this book for information about issues relating to this topic and guidance for structuring this type of essay.

The following steps are suggestions on how to get started.

Step One: Choose your topic.

The first step is to decide what topic to write your expository essay on. Is there anything that particularly fascinates you about racial profiling, racism, security, or civil liberties? Is there an aspect of the topic you strongly support, or feel strongly against? Is there an issue you feel personally connected to or one that you would like to learn more about? Ask yourself such questions before selecting your essay topic. Refer to Appendix D: Sample Essay Topics if you need help selecting a topic.

Step Two: Write down questions and answers about the topic.

Before you begin writing, you will need to think carefully about what ideas your essay will contain. This is a process known as *brainstorming*. Brainstorming involves asking yourself questions and coming up with ideas to discuss in your essay. Possible questions that will help you with the brainstorming process include:

- Why is this topic important?
- Why should people be interested in this topic?
- How can I make this essay interesting to the reader?
- What question am I going to address in this paragraph or essay?
- What facts, ideas, or quotes can I use to support the answer to my question?

Questions especially for persuasive essays include:

- Do I want to write an informative essay or an opinionated essay?

- Will I need to explain a process or course of action?
- Will my essay contain many definitions or explanations?
- Is there a particular problem that needs to be solved?

Step Three: Gather facts, ideas, and anecdotes related to your topic.

This book contains several places to find information about many aspects of racial profiling, including the viewpoints and the appendices. In addition, you may want to research the books, articles, and websites listed in Section Three, or do additional research in your local library. You can also conduct interviews if you know someone who has a compelling story that would fit well in your essay.

Step Four: Develop a workable, thesis statement.

Use what you have written down in steps two and three to help you articulate the main point or argument you want to make in your essay. It should be expressed in a clear sentence and make an arguable or supportable point.

Example:

Discrimination makes poor police work.

This could be the thesis statement of an essay that argues that racial profiling is discriminatory, ineffective, and even anti-American.

Step Five: Write an outline or diagram.

1. Write the thesis statement at the top of the outline.
2. Write roman numerals I, II, and III on the left side of the page with A, B, and C under each numeral.
3. Next to each roman numeral, write down the best ideas you came up with in step three. These should all directly relate to and support the thesis statement.
4. Next to each letter write down information that supports that particular idea.

Step Six: Write the three supporting paragraphs.

Use your outline to write the three supporting paragraphs. Write down the main idea of each paragraph in sentence form. Do the same thing for the supporting points of information. Each sentence should support the paragraph of the topic. Be sure you have relevant and interesting details, facts, and quotes. Use transitions when you move from idea to idea to keep the text fluid and smooth. Sometimes, although not always, paragraphs can include a concluding or summary sentence that restates the paragraph's argument.

Step Seven: Write the introduction and conclusion.

See Exercise 3B for information on writing introductions and conclusions.

Step Eight: Read and rewrite.

As you read, check your essay for the following:

- ✔ Does the essay maintain a consistent tone?
- ✔ Do all paragraphs reinforce your general thesis?
- ✔ Do all paragraphs flow from one to the other, or do you need to add transition words or phrases?
- ✔ Have you quoted from reliable, authoritative, and interesting sources?
- ✔ Is there a sense of progression throughout the essay?
- ✔ Does the essay get bogged down in too much detail or irrelevant material?
- ✔ Does your introduction grab the reader's attention?
- ✔ Does your conclusion reflect back on any previously discussed material or give the essay a sense of closure?
- ✔ Are there any spelling or grammatical errors?

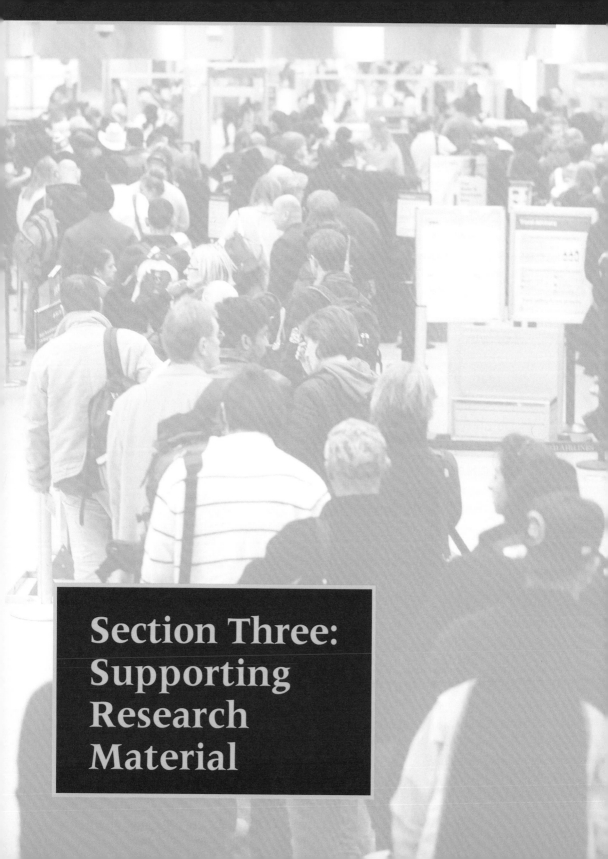

**Section Three:
Supporting
Research
Material**

Facts About Racial Profiling

Editor's Note: These facts can be used in reports to reinforce or add credibility when making important points or claims.

Racial Profiling Laws

According to the Racial Profiling Data Collection Resource Center at Northeastern University, as of January 2012:

- Twenty-eight states have passed legislation prohibiting racial profiling and/or requiring jurisdictions within the state to collect data on law enforcement stops and searches. These include: Arkansas, California, Colorado, Connecticut, Florida, Illinois, Kansas, Kentucky, Louisiana, Maryland, Massachusetts, Minnesota, Missouri, Montana, Nebraska, Nevada, New Jersey, North Carolina, Oklahoma, Oregon, Rhode Island, South Dakota, Tennessee, Texas, Utah, Virginia, Washington, and West Virginia.
- Five states have such legislation pending: Alabama, Georgia, Indiana, New York, and Pennsylvania.
- Seventeen states and the District of Columbia have no such legislation: Alaska, Arizona, Delaware, Hawaii, Idaho, New Mexico, North Dakota, Iowa, Maine, Michigan, Mississippi, Ohio, New Hampshire, South Carolina, Vermont, Wisconsin, and Wyoming.

According to the Center for Immigration Studies:

Arizona Senate Bill 1070, which became state law in 2010, includes the following provisions:

- Aliens (noncitizens) are required to register and carry their documents with them at all times.
- Violating federal immigration law is a state crime in addition to a federal one.

- Police are allowed to ask about immigration status in the normal course of "lawful contact" with a person, such as a traffic stop or if they have committed a crime.
- Before asking a person about immigration status, law enforcement officials are required by the law to have "reasonable suspicion" that a person is an illegal immigrant. Examples of legal reasonable suspicion include:
  - A driver stopped for a traffic violation has no license, or record of a driver's license or other form of federal or state identification.
  - A police officer sees someone buying fake identity documents or crossing the border illegally.
  - A police officer recognizes a gang member known to have been previously deported.
  - The law specifically states that police "may not solely consider race, color or national origin" during such stops.

According to the Leadership Conference on Civil and Human Rights:
- On June 6, 2001, Russell Feingold, a Democratic senator from Wisconsin, and John Conyers, a Democratic representative from Michigan, introduced the End Racial Profiling Act of 2001 (ERPA 2001) into the 107th Congress, which sought to make racial profiling officially illegal.
- In the wake of the September 11 terrorist acts, however, it failed to pass, due to concerns that racial profiling was necessary to national security in the new post-9/11 era.
- Subsequent End Racial Profiling Acts were introduced into Congress in 2004, 2005, 2007, and 2009, but they also did not pass.
- In July 2010 the End Racial Profiling Act of 2010 (ERPA 2010) was again introduced, but Congress

took no action on it, and it died when Congress adjourned that December.

Studies About Racial Profiling

According to the Racial Profiling Data Collection Resource Center at Northeastern University, in 2006 the New York City Police Department (NYPD) stopped a half-million pedestrians for suspected criminal involvement. Raw statistics for these encounters suggest 89 percent of the stops involved nonwhites.

A 2009 study by William Press, a bioinformatics researcher at the University of Texas, Austin, and at Los Alamos National Laboratories, undertook a mathematical analysis of how security profiles are deployed. The results, which were published in the *Proceedings of the National Academies of Science,* concluded that racial profiling is no more effective than random screening.

A study conducted by the Rand Corporation analyzed 7,607 vehicle stops made between June and December 2003 in Oakland, California. The study found that black drivers composed 54 percent of the stops at night and 50 percent of stops during the day. The difference is not statistically significant and overall did not support evidence of racial profiling. However, the study did find indications that racial disparities occur during post-stop activities, including how long stops took, frequency of pat searches, and whether a citation was issued.

Between 2002 and 2005, the Department of Justice and the Bureau of Justice Statistics tracked the rates of routine traffic stops. They found that white, black and Hispanic drivers had about an even chance—between 8.1 and 9.2 percent—of being stopped by police. Yet white drivers were much less likely to be subjected to a search: Of the white drivers stopped, only 3.5 to 3.6 percent of them were searched. On the other hand, 9.5 to 10.2 percent of black drivers were searched, while 8.8 to 11.4 percent of Hispanic drivers were searched.

Americans' Opinions About Racial Profiling*

A December 2009 Rasmussen poll found that 63 percent of Americans think security precautions put in place after 9/11 are "not too much of a hassle."

A June 2010 ABC News/*Washington Post* poll asked Americans whether they supported Arizona's SB 1070, which gives police the power to ask people they have stopped to verify their residency status:
- 58 percent said they supported the law;
- 41 percent said they opposed the law; and
- 2 percent were unsure.

A July 2010 CNN/Opinion Research Corporation poll found the following about American opinions regarding Arizona's immigration law:
- 48 percent said it will reduce illegal immigration;
- 50 percent said it will not reduce illegal immigration; and
- 2 percent were unsure;

- 54 percent said it will lead to discrimination against Hispanics;
- 44 percent said it will not lead to discrimination against Hispanics; and
- 2 percent said they were unsure.

A CBS News/*New York Times* poll conducted in 2010 asked Americans how likely they thought it was that Arizona's SB 1070 would lead police officers to detain people of certain racial or ethnic groups more frequently than those of other racial or ethnic groups. The following responses were obtained:
- 50 percent said "very likely";
- 32 percent said "somewhat likely";
- 11 percent said "not too likely";
- 4 percent said "not at all likely"; and
- 3 percent were unsure;

- 32 percent of Republicans said "very likely";
- 46 percent of Republicans said "somewhat likely";
- 17 percent of Republicans said "not too likely";
- 3 percent of Republicans said "not at all likely"; and
- 2 percent of Republicans said they were unsure;

- 63 percent of Democrats said "very likely";
- 29 percent of Democrats said "somewhat likely";
- 5 percent of Democrats said "not too likely";
- 2 percent of Democrats said "not at all likely"; and
- 1 percent of Democrats said they were unsure;

- 51 percent of Independents said "very likely";
- 25 percent of Independents said "somewhat likely";
- 13 percent of Independents said "not too likely";
- 7 percent of Independents said "not at all likely"; and
- 4 percent said they were unsure.

A November 2010 ABC News/*Washington Post* poll asked Americans whether they would support or oppose the Transportation Security Administration's profiling of people and its using available information about passengers in order to determine who gets selected for extra security screening at airports:
- 70 percent supported this security approach;
- 25 percent opposed it; and
- 6 percent were unsure.

*Note: Some poll results add up to 101 because of rounding.

Finding and Using Sources of Information

No matter what type of essay you are writing, it is necessary to find information to support your point of view. You can use sources such as books, magazine articles, newspaper articles, and online articles.

Using Books and Articles

You can find books and articles in a library by using the library's computer or cataloging system. If you are not sure how to use these resources, ask a librarian to help you. You can also use a computer to find many magazine articles and other articles written specifically for the Internet.

You are likely to find a lot more information than you can possibly use in your essay, so your first task is to narrow it down to what is likely to be most usable. Look at book and article titles. Look at book chapter titles and examine the book's index to see if it contains information on the specific topic you want to write about. For example, if you want to write about racial profiling and you find a book about airport security, check the chapter titles and index to be sure it contains information about issues relating to racial profiling before you bother to check out the book.

For a five-paragraph essay, you do not need a great deal of supporting information, so quickly try to narrow down your materials to a few good books and magazine or Internet articles. You do not need dozens. You might even find that one or two good books or articles contain all the information you need.

You probably do not have time to read an entire book, so find the chapters or sections that relate to your topic and skim these. When you find useful information, copy it onto a note card or into a notebook. You should look for supporting facts, statistics, quotations, and examples.

Using the Internet

When you select your supporting information, it is important that you evaluate its source. This is especially important with information you find on the Internet. Because nearly anyone can put information on the Internet, there is as much bad information as good information. Before using Internet information—or any information—try to determine whether the source is reliable. Is the author or Internet site sponsored by a legitimate organization? Is it from a government source? Does the author have any special knowledge or training relating to the topic you are looking up? Does the article give any indication of where its information comes from?

Using Your Supporting Information

When you use supporting information from a book, article, interview, or other source, there are three important things to remember:

1. *Make it clear whether you are using a direct quotation or a paraphrase.* If you copy information directly from your source, you are quoting it. You must put quotation marks around the information and tell where the information comes from. If you put the information in your own words, you are paraphrasing it.

2. *Use the information fairly.* Be careful to use supporting information in the way the author intended it. For example, it is unfair to quote an author as saying, "Racial profiling is very rare" when he or she intended to say, "Many people believe that racial profiling is very rare, but they are wrong." This is called taking information out of context and is using supporting evidence unfairly.

3. *Give credit where credit is due.* Giving credit is known as citing. You must use citations when you use someone else's information, but not every piece of supporting information needs a citation.

- If the supporting information is general knowledge—that is, it can be found in many sources—you do not have to cite your source; for example, "The earth is 93 million miles from the sun." This is general knowledge and can be found in many sources.
- If you directly quote a source, you must cite it.
- If you paraphrase information from a specific source, you must cite it.

If you do not use citations where you should, you are *plagiarizing*—or stealing—someone else's work.

Citing Your Sources

There are a number of ways to cite your sources. Your teacher will probably want you to do it in one of three ways:

- Informal: As in the examples in the model essays presented in Section Two of this book, when you use outside information in your essay, tell where you got the information as part of the text of your essay.
- Informal list: At the end of your essay, place an unnumbered list of all the sources you used. This tells the reader where, in general, your information came from.
- Formal: Use numbered footnotes or endnotes. Footnotes appear at the bottom of the page they appear on whereas endnotes are placed at the end of an article or essay, although they may be placed elsewhere depending on your teacher's requirements.

Using MLA Style to Create a Works Cited List

You will probably need to create a list of works cited for your paper. These include materials that you quoted from, relied heavily on, or consulted to write your paper. There are several different ways to structure these references. The following examples are based on Modern Language Association (MLA) style, one of the major citation styles used by writers.

Book Entries

For most book entries you will need the author's name, the book's title, where it was published, what company published it, and the year it was published. This information is usually found on the title and copyright pages of the book. Variations on book entries include the following:

A book by a single author:
> Axworthy, Michael. *A History of Iran: Empire of the Mind.* New York: Basic Books, 2008.

Two or more books by the same author:
> Pollan, Michael. *In Defense of Food: An Eater's Manifesto.* New York: Penguin, 2009.
> ———. *The Omnivore's Dilemma.* New York: Penguin, 2006.

A book by two or more authors:
> Ronald, Pamela C., and R.W. Adamchak. *Tomorrow's Table: Organic Farming, Genetics, and the Future of Food.* New York: Oxford University Press, 2008.

A book with an editor:
> Friedman, Lauri S., ed. *Introducing Issues with Opposing Viewpoints: War.* Detroit: Greenhaven, 2009.

Periodical and Newspaper Entries

Entries for sources found in periodicals and newspapers are cited a bit differently from books. For one, these sources usually have a title and a publication name. They also may have specific dates and page numbers. Unlike book entries, you do not need to list where newspapers or periodicals are published or what company publishes them.

An article from a periodical:
> Hannum, William H., Gerald E. Marsh, and George S. Stanford. "Smarter Use of Nuclear Waste," *Scientific American* Dec. 2005: 84–91.

An unsigned article from a periodical:
> "Chinese disease? The rapid spread of syphilis in China." *Global Agenda* 14 Jan. 2007.

An article from a newspaper:
> Weiss, Rick. "Can Food from Cloned Animals Be Called Organic?" *Washington Post* 29 Jan. 2008: A06.

Internet Sources

To document a source you found online, try to provide as much information on it as possible so your reader can also find it, including the author's name, the title of the document, date of publication or of last revision, the URL, and your date of access.

An internet source:

> De Seno, Tommy. *"Roe vs. Wade* and the Rights of the Father." The Fox Forum.com 22 Jan. 2009. < http: //foxforum.blogs.foxnews.com/2009/01/22/dese no_roe_wade/ > Accessed May 20, 2009.

Your teacher will tell you exactly how information should be cited in your essay. Generally, the very least information needed is the original author's name and the name of the article or the publication.

Be sure you know exactly what citation information your teacher requires before you start looking for your supporting information so that you know what such information to include with your notes.

Sample Essay Topics on Racial Profiling

Racial Profiling Is a Serious Problem

Racial Profiling Is Not a Serious Problem

Racial Profiling Violates People's Civil Liberties

Opponents of Racial Profiling Sacrifice Security for Political Correctness

Racial Profiling Is Discriminatory and Unfair

Minorities Should Accept Racial Profiling as Necessary for the Greater Good

Racial Profiling Prevents Terrorism

Racial Profiling Does Not Prevent Terrorism

Racial Profiling Improves Security

Racial Profiling Wastes Resources

Racial Profiling Is Lazy Police Work

Racial Profiling Is Targeted Police Work

Police Should Profile Behavior, Not Race

Arizona's SB 1070 Invites Racial Profiling

Arizona's SB 1070 Does Not Invite Racial Profiling

Racial Profiling Helps Prevent Illegal Immigration

Racial Profiling Violates Immigrants' Constitutional Rights

SB 1070 Should Be Adopted by Other States

SB 1070 Should Not Be Adopted by Other States

Topics for Expository Essays

How SB 1070 Became a Law

Defining Racial Profiling

Racial Profiling Can Solve the Problem of "Few Resources, Many Suspects"

Examples of Racial Profiling

The Myth of Racial Profiling

Balancing Civil Liberties with Sound Security

The Problem of "Driving While Black"

The Myth of "Driving While Black"

The Problem of "Flying While Arab"

The Myth of "Flying While Arab"

The Problem of "Walking While Latino"

The Myth of "Walking While Latino"

Profiling and the Case of Israel

Organizations to Contact

The editor has compiled the following list of organizations concerned with the issues debated in this book. The descriptions are derived from materials provided by the organizations. All have publications or information available for interested readers. The list was compiled on the date of publication of the present volume; the information provided here may change. Be aware that many organizations take several weeks or longer to respond to queries, so allow as much time as possible.

American-Arab Anti-Discrimination Committee (ADC)

4201 Connecticut Ave. NW, Ste. 300, Washington, DC 20008
(202) 244-2990
e-mail: adc@adc.org • website: www.adc.org

This organization fights anti-Arab stereotyping in the media and works to protect Arab Americans from discrimination, racial profiling, and hate crimes. It publishes a bimonthly newsletter, the *Chronicle*; issue papers and special reports; community studies; legal, media, and educational guides; and action alerts.

American Civil Liberties Union (ACLU)

125 Broad St., 18th Fl., New York, NY 10004
(212) 549-2500 • fax: (212) 549-2646
website: www.aclu.org

The ACLU is a national organization that works to defend Americans' civil rights as guaranteed by the US Constitution. The ACLU publishes and distributes policy statements, pamphlets, and the semiannual newsletter *Civil Liberties Alert*. It strongly opposes racial profiling.

American Enterprise Institute (AEI)

1150 Seventeenth St. NW
Washington, DC 20036
(202) 862-5800 • fax: (202) 862-7177
e-mail: webmaster@aei.org • website: www.aei.org

The American Enterprise Institute for Public Policy Research is a private, nonprofit, conservative think tank dedicated to research and education on issues of government, politics, economics, and social welfare. It provides policy makers with ideas to meet today's challenges based on the principles of private liberty, free enterprise, and individual opportunity. The AEI's Legal Center for the Public Interest focuses on constitutional research in an effort to preserve the liberties guaranteed in the Constitution.

Arab-American Action Network (AAAN)

3148 W. Sixty-Third St. Chicago, IL 60629
(773) 436-6060 • fax: (773) 436-6460
e-mail: info@aaan.org • website: www.aaan.org

This group strives to strengthen the Arab community by building its capacity to be an active agent for positive social change. As a grassroots nonprofit organization, its strategies include community organizing, advocacy, education, providing social services, leadership development, cultural outreach, and forging productive relationships with other communities.

Cato Institute

1000 Massachusetts Ave. NW, Washington, DC 20001-5403
(202) 842-0200 • fax: (202) 842-3490
e-mail: cato@cato.org • website: www.cato.org

The Cato Institute is a libertarian public policy research foundation dedicated to limiting the role of government and protecting individual liberties. It researches claims of discrimination and racial profiling among many other issues.

Center for Equal Opportunity

7700 Leesburg Pike, Ste. 231
Falls Church, VA 22043
(703) 442-0066
website: www.ceousa.org

The Center for Equal Opportunity supports colorblind public policies and seeks to block the expansion of racial preferences and to prevent their use in employment, education, voting, and police work. It publishes numerous documents on affirmative action, immigration, voting, and other issues.

Center for Immigration Studies

1522 K St. NW, Ste. 820, Washington, DC 20005-1202
(202) 466-8185
e-mail: center@cis.org • website: www.cis.org

The Center for Immigration Studies is the nation's only think tank dedicated to research and analysis of the economic, social, and demographic impacts of immigration on the United States. The center supports immigration policy that is both pro-immigrant and low-immigration. It approves of Arizona's SB 1070, which allows police to ascertain the resident status of people they stop for other issues.

Center for the Study of Popular Culture (CSPC)

9911 W. Pico Blvd., Ste. 1290, Los Angeles, CA 90035
(310) 843-3699 • fax: (310) 843-3692
website: www.cspc.org

CSPC is a conservative educational organization that addresses topics such as political correctness, cultural diversity, discrimination, and racial profiling. Its civil rights project promotes equal opportunity for all individuals and provides legal assistance to citizens.

Citizens' Commission on Civil Rights (CCCR)

2000 M St. NW, Ste. 400, Washington, DC 20036
(202) 659-5565 • fax: (202) 223-5302
e-mail: citizens@cccr.org • website: www.cccr.org

CCCR monitors the federal government's enforcement of antidiscrimination laws and promotes equal opportunity for all. It publishes reports on a variety of racial issues.

Commission for Racial Justice (CRJ)
700 Prospect Ave., Cleveland, OH 44115-1110
(216) 736-2100 • fax: (216) 736-2171

CRJ was formed in 1963 by the United Church of Christ in response to racial tensions gripping the nation at that time. Its goal is a peaceful, dignified society where all men and women of all races and ethnicities are equal. CRJ publishes various documents and books, some of which discuss racial profiling.

Council on American-Islamic Relations (CAIR)
453 New Jersey Ave. SE, Washington, DC 20003
(202) 488-8787 • fax: (202) 488-0833
e-mail: cair@cair-net.org • website: www.cair-net.org

CAIR is a nonprofit membership organization that presents an Islamic perspective to public policy issues and challenges the misrepresentation of Islam and Muslims. It fights discrimination against Muslims in America and lobbies political leaders on issues related to Islam. Its publications include the quarterly newsletter *CAIR News*, reports on Muslim civil rights issues, and periodic action alerts.

Federation for American Immigration Reform
25 Massachusetts Ave NW, Ste. 330
Washington, DC 20001
(202) 328-7004 • fax: (202) 387-3447
website: www.fairus.org

FAIR seeks to improve border security, stop illegal immigration, and promote immigration laws it believes will serve these ends. It supports Arizona's SB 1070 and other aggressive laws aimed at curbing illegal immigration.

The Heritage Foundation

214 Massachusetts Ave. NE, Washington, DC 20002-4999
(202) 546-4400 • fax: (202) 546-8328
e-mail: info@heritage.org • website: www.heritage.org

The foundation is a conservative public policy research institute that advocates free-market principles, individual liberty, and limited government. It believes the private sector, not government, should ease social problems and help improve the status of minorities.

Institute for Justice

901 N. Glebe Rd., Ste. 900
Arlington, VA 22203
(703) 682-9320 • fax: (703) 682-9321
e-mail: general@ij.org • website: www.ij.org

The Institute for Justice is a libertarian public interest law firm providing litigation and advocacy on behalf of individuals whose most basic rights have been violated by the government. It works to secure economic liberty, private property rights, and freedom of speech for all members of society, and it aims to restore constitutional limits on the power of government. Its publications include a bimonthly newsletter, various reports, articles, and papers on various liberty interests.

National Network for Immigrant and Refugee Rights (NNIRR)

310 Eighth St., Ste. 307, Oakland, CA 94607
(510) 465-1984 • fax: (510) 465-1885
e-mail: nnirrinfo@nnirr.org • website: www.nnirr.org

The NNIRR includes community, church, labor, and legal groups committed to the cause of equal rights for all immigrants. These groups work to end discrimination and unfair treatment of illegal immigrants and refugees. The network publishes a monthly newsletter, *Network News*.

National Security Agency (NSA)
9800 Savage Rd.
Ft. George Meade, MD 20755
(301) 688-6524 • fax: (301) 688-6198
website: www.nsa.gov

The NSA is an intelligence agency administered by the US Department of Defense. Its main goal is to protect national security systems and to produce foreign intelligence information. The NSA follows US laws to defeat terrorist organizations at home and abroad and ensures the protection of privacy and civil liberties of American citizens. Speeches, congressional testimonies, press releases, and research reports are all available on the NSA website.

National Urban League
120 Wall St., 8th Fl., New York, NY 10005
(212) 558-5300 • fax: (212) 344-5332
website: www.nul.org

A community service agency, the National Urban League aims to eliminate institutional racism in the United States. It also provides services for minorities who experience discrimination in employment, housing, welfare, and other areas. It publishes the report *The Price: A Study of the Costs of Racism in America* and the annual *State of Black America*.

Southern Poverty Law Center
400 Washington Ave.
Montgomery, AL 36104
(334) 956-8200
website: www.splcenter.org

The Southern Poverty Law Center is a nonprofit civil rights organization dedicated to fighting hate and bigotry and to seeking justice for the most vulnerable members of society. It has produced numerous reports and documents about racial profiling that will be useful to students.

United States Department of Homeland Security (DHS)

Washington, DC 20528
(202) 282-8000
e-mail: multimedia@dhs.gov • website: www.dhs.gov

The Department of Homeland Security was created after the September 11, 2001, terrorist attacks to secure the nation while preserving American freedoms and liberties. It is charged with protecting the United States from terrorists, decreasing the country's vulnerability to terrorism, and effectively responding to attacks. The current DHS homeland security strategic plan can be found on its website.

United States Department of Justice (DOJ)

950 Pennsylvania Ave. NW,
Washington, DC 20530-0001
(202) 514-2000
e-mail: askdoj@usdoj.gov • website: www.usdoj.gov

The DOJ functions to enforce the law and defend the interests of the United States. Its primary duties are to ensure public safety against foreign and domestic threats, to provide federal leadership in preventing and controlling crime, to seek just punishment for those guilty of unlawful behavior, to administer and enforce the nation's immigration laws fairly and effectively, and to ensure fair and impartial administration of justice for all Americans.

Bibliography

Books

Katherine Benton-Cohen, *Borderline Americans: Racial Division and Labor War in the Arizona Borderlands.* Cambridge, MA: Harvard University Press, 2011.

Alejandro del Carmen, *Racial Profiling in America.* Englewood Cliffs, NJ: Prentice Hall, 2007.

Joseph Collum, *The Black Dragon: Racial Profiling Exposed.* Sun River, MT: Jigsaw Press, 2010.

Susan N. Herman, *Taking Liberties: The War on Terror and the Erosion of American Democracy.* New York: Oxford University Press, 2011.

Periodicals and Internet Sources

Arizona Daily Star, "Racial Profiling, SB 1070 Will Go Hand in Hand," April 16, 2010. http://azstarnet.com/news /opinion/editorial/article_a10573e6-03dd-5c13-b345 -a84a74fb47ed.html.

Debra Burlingame, "U.S. Airports Should Use Racial and Religious Profiling," Intelligence Squared U.S., Rosenkranz Foundation, November 22, 2010, p. 3–5. http://intelligencesquaredus.org/wp-content/uploads /airport-profiling-112210.pdf.

Arian Campo-Flores, "Arizona's Immigration Law and Racial Profiling," *Newsweek,* April 26, 2010.

Marcia Alesan Dawkins, "Driving While Black, Flying While Arab, Walking While Latino," *AlterNet,* June 9, 2010. http://blogs.alternet.org/speakeasy/2010/06/09 /deterred-and-discouraged.

Chauncey DeVega, "A Reminder That Whiteness Is Not Benign: Of Warnings About White, Middle Class Domestic Terrorists in the U.S. and the Norway Massacre," *AlterNet,* July 28, 2011. http://blogs.alter

net.org/speakeasy/2011/07/28/a-reminder-that
-whiteness-is-not-benign-of-warnings-about-white
-middle-class-domestic-terrorists-in-the-u-s-and-the
-norway-massacre.

Palash R. Ghosh, "Will Blonde-Haired, Blue-Eyed White Men Now Be Racially Profiled?," *International Business Times,* July 25, 2011. www.ibtimes.com/articles /186297/20110725/oslo-norway-terrorism-murder -profiling-racial-anders-behring-breivik.htm.

Holland (MI) Sentinel, "Arizona-Style Immigration Law Would Invite Racial Profiling," March 11, 2010. www .hollandsentinel.com/opinions/x1777799364/OUR -VIEW-Arizona-style-immigration-law-would-invite -racial-profiling.

Arsalan Iftikhar, "Why Profiling Doesn't Work," CNN .com, January 5, 2010. http://articles.cnn.com/2010 -01-05/opinion/iftikhar.profiling.does.not.work_1 _profiling-security-risk-airliner?_s = PM:OPINION.

Jerusalem Post, "Keep Our Airports Safe," March 9, 2011. www.jpost.com/Opinion/Editorials/Article.asp x?id = 211484.

Kris W. Kobach, "Why Arizona Had to Draw a Line on Illegal Immigrants," *New York Times,* April 28, 2010. www.nytimes.com/2010/04/29/opinion/29kobach .html.

The Leadership Conference, *Restoring a National Consensus: The Need to End Racial Profiling in America,* March 2011. www.civilrights.org/publications/reports/racial-pro filing2011/racial_profiling2011.pdf.

Andrew C. McCarthy, "So, We Should Profile When It Helps Muslims?," *National Review,* July 22, 2011. www .nationalreview.com/corner/272577/so-we-should -profile-when-it-helps-muslims-andrew-c-mccarthy.

Robert J. Meadows, "The Case for Racial Profiling," *Ventura County Star* (CA), July 24, 2010. www.vcstar .com/news/2010/jul/24/the-case-for-racial-profiling /%3Fpartner = RSS.

New York Times, "Will Profiling Make a Difference?,"
January 4, 2010. http://roomfordebate.blogs.nytimes
.com/2010/01/04/will-profiling-make-a-difference.

Dean Obeidallah, "(Not) Flying While Muslim,"
Huffington Post, January 2, 2009. www.huffington
post.com/dean-obeidallah/not-flying-while-muslim
_b_154872.html.

Brian Palmer, "What's So Great About Israeli Security?,"
Slate, January 3, 2011. www.slate.com/id/2279753
/?from = rss.

Robert Parry, "Who Commits Terrorism?," OpEd News,
July 27, 2011. www.opednews.com/articles/5/Who
-Commits-Terrorism-by-Robert-Parry-110727-810
.html.

Anshel Pfeffer, "In Israel, Racial Profiling Doesn't Warrant
Debate, or Apologies," Haaretz.com, January 8, 2010.
www.haaretz.com/print-edition/news/in-israel-racial
-profiling-doesn-t-warrant-debate-or-apologies-1
.261075.

Nafees A. Sayed, "Airport Screening for 'Flying While
Muslim,'" CNN.com, January 29, 2010. http://articles
.cnn.com/2010-01-29/opinion/syed.muslim.while
.flying_1_profiling-muslim-women-head-scarf?_s
= PM:OPINION.

Seattle Times, "Arizona's Unhelpful New Immigration Law
Invites Racial Profiling," April 26, 2010. http://seattle
times.nwsource.com/html/editorials/2011709679
_edit27immigration.html.

Seattle Times, "Flying While Muslim—a Case of Intolerable
Discrimination," May 11, 2011. http://seattletimes
.nwsource.com/html/editorials/2015028256_edit12
islam.html.

Ralph Stone, "Racial Profiling and Arizona's New
Immigration Law," *California Progress Report,* April
30, 2010. www.californiaprogressreport.com/site
/node/7709.

Websites

Flying While Muslim (www.flyingwhilemuslim.org) This site was created after six imams (Muslim clerics) were removed from a US Airways flight in March 2007. It offers breaking updates on their case and links to organizations and websites that cover racial profiling–related news.

Muslims for a Safe America (http://muslimsforasafeamerica.org) The goal of this site is to educate American Muslims on a variety of national security issues, including racial profiling.

National Conference of State Legislatures, Analysis of Arizona's Immigration Law (www.ncsl.org/?tabid = 20263) A good overview of SB 1070 with links to relevant legislative documents. A good primary source for reports.

Racial Profiling Data Collection Resource Center at Northeastern University (www.racialprofilinganalysis.neu.edu) Part of the Institute on Race and Justice at Northeastern University, this website uses social science research methods to assist government agencies, educational institutions, and members of the private sector with development, enhancement, and implementation of contemporary criminal justice policies and issues. The website spotlights racial profiling incidents and has a comprehensive legislation section that will be useful to students.

Index

Picture Credits

About the Editor

Lauri S. Scherer earned her bachelor's degree in religion and political science from Vassar College in Poughkeepsie, New York. Her studies there focused on political Islam. Scherer has worked as a nonfiction writer, a newspaper journalist, and a book editor for more than ten years. She has extensive experience in both academic and professional settings.

Scherer is the founder of LSF Editorial, a writing and editing company in San Diego. She has edited and authored numerous publications for Greenhaven Press on controversial social issues such as Islam, genetically modified food, women's rights, school shootings, gay marriage, and Iraq. Every book in the *Writing the Critical Essay* series has been under her direction or editorship, and she has personally written more than twenty titles in the series. She was instrumental in the creation of the series and played a critical role in its conception and development.

HV
7936
.R3
R35
2012

Racial profiling.

DATE			